SO-AEL-074

Religion in Human Life
Anthropological Views

EDWARD NORBECK
Rice University

WAVELAND
PRESS, INC.
Prospect Heights, Illinois

For information about this book, write or call:

Waveland Press, Inc.
P.O. Box 400
Prospect Heights, Illinois 60070
(312) 634-0081

Copyright © 1974 by Holt, Rinehart and Winston, Inc.
1988 reissued by Waveland Press, Inc.

ISBN 0-88133-354-9

All rights reserved. No part of this book may be reproduced, stored in a retrieval system, or transmitted in any form or by any means without permission in writing from the publisher.

Printed in the United States of America

Foreword

THE AUTHOR

Edward Norbeck was born on a wilderness homestead in Canada at the northern edge of the Great Plains and became a naturalized citizen of the United States in Hawaii. After earlier degrees at the University of Michigan in oriental languages and civilizations, he received his doctoral training in anthropology at that university. He is the author, editor, or co-editor of fourteen books on a wide range of anthropological subjects that, in addition to religion, include Japanese society and culture, Hawaii, the study of human play, the formation of human personality, and archeology. His field research has been principally in Japan and Hawaii, but his interests in ways of human life have taken him to many foreign countries as well as most of the United States. His regular professorial post from 1960 until his retirement in 1981 was at Rice University, where he also held various administrative appointments. After official retirement from Rice University, he taught for five additional years at other universities as visiting professor, as he also had done earlier during summers and while on sabbatical leave. Thus, like his interests in the human world, his teaching has taken him to many places, a total of 12 universities in the United States, Canada, and Japan.

THIS UNIT

Religion in human life certainly qualifies as a basic topic for this series. It is not an easy subject to treat effectively in brief compass. Edward Norbeck has done so gracefully and informatively. He develops two themes: the description of religious events, rituals, and states of mind; and the nature of anthropological aims, views, procedures, and interpretations. The interweaving of these two themes provides a view of religion as an anthropological subject and of religion as a process in human life that is unexpected in this short book. Instructors of anthropology familiar with anthropological writing on religion will find that the author has not only touched upon many standard topics included in the study of religion, but has also included treatments of material not ordinarily covered in standard anthropological works, such as "etiquette and religion," "religion and human play," "rites of reversal," and certain aspects of "religious transcendence."

George and Louise Spindler

Contents

PART I

Introduction:
The Anthropological
Study of Religion

1
The Nature of Religion:
Anthropological Views

Pioneers in anthropology observed long ago that religion is universal among human societies. Nonreligious individuals have become common enough in the modern world, but religious beliefs continue to be held and upheld in all societies. After the sixteenth century, Europeans who spread throughout the world had no difficulty in recognizing beliefs and acts of supernaturalism even in the societies most remote from them in world views and ways of life. These were usually described as outlandish and inferior practices of heathens and, often enough, dismissed from further consideration. The growth of science and the emergence of anthropology in the nineteenth century set aside the appraisal of inferiority and looked upon the customs as human behavior worthy of objective study aimed toward gaining an understanding of the nature of man. The modern scholarly problem has then been one of finding ways to make these and all other customs of religion comprehensible.

FORMS OF RELIGIOUS BEHAVIOR

Foreign beliefs and acts of religion are often puzzling. They frequently appear to have no recognizable counterparts in our own religious customs, and native statements of the reasons for the practices often fail to provide acceptable explanations of their goals or sometimes even of the manifest reasons for their existence beyond the blind following of tradition. The anthropological study of religion has sought to see rhyme and reason in these customs as well as in other human behavior, and has offered interpretations of their role in human life and of the factors that have molded the customs into their particular forms.

But let us first have a brief look at a miscellaneous collection of bizarre and puzzling religious beliefs and acts among foreign societies. No interpretations of the significance of the customs by anthropologists will be given at this time. In the chapters that follow, however, such interpretations are explicitly stated or may readily be inferred. The customs described below are chosen principally as representatives of kinds or classes of beliefs and acts, and, in lesser part, because they are unfamiliar.

We see as bizarre the actions of natives of New Hanover Island in the southern Pacific Ocean, who once raised the huge sum of $2,000 to buy Lyndon B. Johnson for use as an intermediary with the supernatural world. We regard as strange, and probably incomprehensible, the custom of the male Fox Indian of aboriginal times of addressing his guardian spirit, the supernatural being of greatest importance to him, as "My Nephew." We also regard as strange various practices of using the form of divination called the ordeal to determine the guilt or innocence of people charged with crimes and other offenses. These customs often appear to allow no chance for the accused to demonstrate innocence, leading us to wonder how the customs might have survived without causing critical social disturbance. In Europe and the United States in bygone days, for example, the ordeal by water was used to judge the guilt or innocence of persons accused of witchcraft: the innocent sank and the guilty floated.

Bizarreness, let us note, is in the eyes of the beholder, and Christian symbolism has often been bizarre to foreign eyes. To Europeans, "Lamb of God" has meaning, but it has no meaning to native Austrialians or Melanesians. However, the suitable Australian and Melanesian counterparts, "Kangaroo of God" and "Pig of God," are absurd, bizarre, and sometimes repulsive to Westerners. A Christian congregation of the United States or Europe would doubtless have the same feelings toward a painting in oriental cast of the Last Supper in which all of the saintly diners have eyes with Mongoloid folds and are using chopsticks.

Rites of passage, ceremonies observed throughout the world that mark the transition from one social status to another, include many themes and specific acts that are not found in modern Western religious practices or have no easily recognizable Western counterparts today. Requirements that people do unusual things are very common during rites of passage of all kinds. A ceremony observed at childbirth in many primitive societies called the *couvade* requires that the mother be separated from the rest of the society and bear her child in seclusion while the father remains with his social group and becomes the center of ritual observances that may include simulation by him of the act of giving birth. With no therapeutic goals whatever, many societies have required as a part of coming-of-age ceremonies the circumcision or other kinds of surgical alteration of the sexual organs of males and sometimes of females. Rites of the Bemba tribe of Northern Rhodesia (now the nation of Zambia) that marked the coming of age of young women required that girls catch water bugs with their mouths. Similar rites in many societies of American Indians of the western United States prohibited girls from scratching their bodies with their fingers during the ritual period. A very common element of rites of marriage of societies of sub-Saharan Africa required the "capture" of the bride by the groom and his relatives. Although the marriage had ordinarily long been arranged to the satisfaction of all concerned, the bride was expected to act reluctant to join the groom, and she and her relatives conducted a dramatic, sham battle of resistance. In the Western view, funeral rites of many societies seem remarkable and inappropriate because they come to an end as joyous celebrations in which the bereaved participate in feasts, dancing, and other pleasurable activities.

To Western eyes perhaps the most remarkable class of rituals commonly found elsewhere in the world is one requiring that some or all persons act in ways that are the reverse of ordinary procedures. Males may be required to wear the clothing of females and females those of males. In some societies, clothing must be donned "backwards" or inside out; dancing must be the "reverse" of the normal. Reversals often extend to moral rules, which may be suspended or reversed to allow or even require obscenity, lewdness, sexual freedom, and the temporary violation of many other rules of behavior with moral import that apply firmly at other times of the year. On these occasions, the acts are all regarded by the people concerned as proper behavior and as a part of religious ceremonial.

ANTHROPOLOGICAL VIEWS OF RELIGION

Anthropological interpretation sees in customs such as those described above much that is held in common, and also usually sees counterparts of them in the customs of our own society, today or in the past. The anthropological study of religion may, in fact, be described as a study of similarities and differences in beliefs and practices throughout the world. As a result of this comparative study, the religions of the world are seen to be fundamentally alike in underlying philosophies, ritual acts, and in the roles which religion plays in human life. Supernatural beings and human behavior toward them are everywhere fundamentally similar. Magical practices of the entire world may all be classified under a small number of categories resting upon a limited range of principles. The times or occasions of ritual observances are also alike everywhere. Where differences occur, these may be seen as reflecting differences in other features of the ways of life, past or present, of the peoples concerned.

During the century since the beginning of anthropology as an organized branch of study, factual knowledge about the religious beliefs and acts of different societies has increased greatly. Methods of study have grown in diversity and refinement, and various theoretical approaches to the interpretation of religion have developed, sometimes waxing for a time and then waning. The growth of anthropological understanding of religion does not, however, stem solely from the efforts of anthropologists but includes considerable adaptive borrowing from other social sciences. Anthropological interpretations of religion are nevertheless distinctive, in part because they rest upon various basic assumptions about the nature of religion that have remained essentially unchanged since their formulation in the infancy of cultural anthropology.

One important source of distinctiveness lies in the objective of cultural anthropology of gaining an understanding of man primarily by examining his culture, the part of his universe which he himself has created. In the anthropological view, then, religion is a creation of man that varies in ways that are congruent with the conditions of life of each society.

As might be expected, most anthropological studies at any point in time have accorded with the lines of theory then prevailing. The origin and evolution of religion were dominant interests at first, to be succeeded for a time largely by histories and inferred histories of religion, and followed still later by an emphasis on studies concerning the relationship of religion to the social order and to other elements of culture. Modern times find all of these interests alive. A rich addition of theories and interests has come from psychology, social psychology, psychiatry, and sociology. The modern social anthropologist, whose interests in religion center upon its relationship to the social order, may wish to distinguish himself in professional title from the cultural anthropologist, whose professional interests are less intensely directed toward social structure and social relations. But eclecticism in theory has become common, and notable trends of unanimity and mutual interest are evident despite the existence of divergent streams of anthropological theory.

One of the subjects of seemingly greatest diversity of opinion in anthropology is the definition of religion, but even in this matter it is possible to see a fair degree of consensus. Religion is characteristically seen by anthropologists as a distinctive symbolic expression of human life that interprets man himself and his universe, providing motives for human action, and also a group of associated acts which have had survival value for the human species.

The point of disagreement has been how to distinguish religious philosophies and acts from other ideas and practices that might be comprehended by this definition but are not ordinarily regarded as religion. Attempts to define religion in the past century have included much scholarly argument concerning distinctions between the supernatural and the natural, the sacred and the profane (which might or might not correspond closely with the concepts of supernaturalism and natural-ism), and distinctions between magic and religion. In recent years, a concept of religion as a set of "ultimate values" has sometimes been expressed. This definition, which came to anthropology from sociology, generally means the ideas and ideals about which human beings feel most keenly. So defined, religion may include, but is not restricted to, ideas of supernaturalism, and also includes political ideology or any other cherished values. According to this definition, religion is presumably a universal attribute of all societies and all individuals. How much currency this view of religion might have among anthropologists is uncertain.

Inference from the contents of published anthropological accounts of religion, however, shows fairly general agreement among anthropologists in the conception of religion used as a basis for practical research. The distinguishing trait commonly used is supernaturalism, ideas and acts centered on views of supernatural power. Concepts of supernaturalism are those involving ideas of supernatural beings with variable powers and also ideas of supernatural power or efficiency that is thought to exist throughout the universe or to inhere in certain objects, substances, and natural phenomena; in some or all human beings and other living forms in variable quantity; and in certain acts. These two ideas have sometimes been called concepts of *personified supernatural power* (the acts or capabilities of supernatural beings with the quality of life) and *impersonal power* (objectlike, inanimate power). To be sure, various primitive societies of the world do not seem clearly to distinguish the supernatural from the natural, and the anthropological use of the category "supernatural" may be regarded as an ethnocentric projection of the culture of the anthropologists. It is certain, however, that a great many and perhaps most societies, whether primitive or civilized, do distinguish between the natural and the super-natural. It seems reasonable, also, to argue that understanding for the members of our own society or any other society must proceed through the use of concepts that are somehow familiar, if only by analogy. The issue of whether or not a particular society has distinct concepts of the natural and the supernatural has, in fact, been irrelevant to most of the questions that anthropologists have asked and attempted to answer about religion.

The problem of distinguishing religion from magic has been similarly handled in anthropology, and many modern anthropologists do not concern themselves with this matter. To most anthropologists, magic is regarded as supernaturalistic behavior distinguished principally by implying the control of supernatural forces by human beings through mechanical acts, formulas that reach desired "natural" goals if followed properly, and religion implies ideas of and behavior toward supernatural beings with power to do things that affect man. In their effects, both magic and religion are seen as being fundamentally alike. Both are placed under the title of supernaturalism, and interpretation of their significance proceeds along lines that are essentially identical.

The views of anthropology show agreement in various other matters that relate to the study of man and culture as well as to the study of religion. For most purposes no consideration is given to racial differences or to other biological aspects of the human organism. All living varieties of man are looked upon as being sufficiently alike in genetically inherited traits and capabilities so that innate biological factors may and should be omitted from consideration in attempts to answer most anthropological questions. No attempt is made to explain the features of Aztec religion, for example, by recourse to genetically inherited traits of Aztec Indians. Instead, Aztec culture is examined. However, in trying to understand certain traits of culture, such as the social unit of the family, that are universal in human society, it is useful to consider human beings as biological organisms for the reason that the cultural universals might represent responses to organismic or innate needs. Human infants are born helpless and are unable for many years to fend for themselves without the aid of adults. Without a social unit such as the family, human beings could not exist in their present form.

As we have noted, religion is one of the cultural universals. But, it must be added, no clearly defined biological wellspring of religion is evident unless it is the human capacity and proclivity to create culture, to interpret the universe, and to formulate that interpretation in such a way as to make life and perpetuation of the human species possible. The question of whether or not religion is in fact a cultural universal applying to all human beings thus depends upon the definition of religion. Defined as supernaturalism, religion is universal to all societies if not to all individuals.

The preceding sentences indirectly restate another enduring assumption of anthropology, that religious beliefs and acts are created by man on the basis of the circumstances of his life. The ideas of religion—of gods, souls, spirits, ghosts, monsters, witches, and the rest of the international assemblage of supernatural beings, and the deeds they perform—are seen as being eminently manlike, projections on a supernatural plane of the wishes, hopes, fears, tensions, affections, animosities, and capabilities or desired capabilities of man himself. Ideas of impersonal power are seen as being analogous with mundane human experience with objects and their qualities. These concepts interpret the universe and either explicitly include or strongly suggest courses of human action to gain desired ends and maintain well-being. If a powerful deity controls all matters that favor and disfavor mankind, it is important to gain his goodwill by following rules of behavior that please him. If the possession of mysterious, impersonal power is seen as the prerequisite for success in endeavors of life, gaining and controlling such power are obviously desirable.

Like other elements of culture, religious beliefs and acts are viewed as tools that have aided man to survive, and, like other kinds of tools, religious beliefs and practices are variably efficient. They may be seen to have disadvantages as well as advantages, especially when other conditions of life change. Becoming outmoded, they must then either change or become extinct.

Most of these various anthropological ideas of religion may be summed up in somewhat more technical terms in the framework of systems theory. As in other fields of science that use the idea of systems, certain fundamental ideas about the nature of the system called culture (or society, if one is a social anthropologist) exist in anthropology. Systems are wholes composed of interrelated parts in states of equilibrium or homeostasis; that is, in compatible functional relationship. Any given state of equilibrium (arrangement of parts of the system and the relations of these parts to one another and to the whole system) remains theoretically constant until or unless change in any significant part comes about by whatever means. Change may come about as the result of malfunction within the system—the abrasion or weakening of parts by the action of other parts or from outside inter-ference—or change may occur through addition, modification, removal, or dis-placements of parts (in the system called culture, most importantly by invention, discovery, or diffusion of cultural traits with concomitant rearrangements, modifica-tions, and extinctions).

"Functionalist" interpretations of religion have, accordingly, studied the rela-tionships of religion to other elements of culture, most frequently centering their attention on social structure and social relations. Cultural evolutionists have similarly studied relationships of cultural elements with the goal of formulating generalizations about the manner in which culture changes and evolves into new forms.

In the study of religion as well as of other aspects of culture, the procedures of anthropology have been comparative; that is, anthropologists have sought to learn the full range of culture among societies of the world and then to account for similarities and differences that have been noted. Attempts to explain similarities and differences proceed primarily within the boundaries of systems theory with due consideration to the possibility of diffusion from one society to another, against the background of the knowledge that man as a biological species has innate needs, capabilities, and limitations to which culture relates directly or indirectly. Whether religious or other elements of culture are established by diffusion from another society or are independent formulations of a particular society, their relations in the cultural system of the society being studied are the primary concern in modern interpretations.

Anthropological investigation of the world has shown remarkable correspondences in culture, correspondences that long ago became so familiar to anthropologists if not to other citizens that they cease to be astounding. In the realm of religion many concepts and ritual events are found everywhere: Ideas of spirits, souls, gods, demons, personalized and impersonal power, rites that celebrate events of importance, and much else. The emphasis in anthropological research in recent years upon attempts to understand the systemic nature of culture has resulted in many studies that seemingly ignore direct consideration of the significance of religion to man. Yet a vast group of publications of the recent past are interpretations of the role of religion in human life, and most studies easily allow inference of this kind. For a period of two decades or longer beginning in the 1930s, many anthropological studies of religion making use of systems theory sought explicitly to relate religion to human life. Decades of earlier thought had pointed to certain obvious effects of religion in these respects, such as the role of religion as a force toward moral conformity and thus toward social harmony; in providing entertainment; and, through beliefs in gods and magical procedures, of providing assurance, reassurance, and solace. Many beliefs and customs were difficult to understand as serving mankind in these ways, however, and certain ideas and practices, such as those of witchcraft, appeared at first glance to be only disruptive to the society and the individual. Interpretation of these and other seemingly less puzzling customs has proceeded by viewing religious beliefs and acts as symbolic blueprints or models that guide the behavior of human beings in ways that are hidden from the view of members of society.

Guided by a form of systems theory that might now be called "early functionalism," these studies sought primarily to see the functions of religion in supporting or maintaining the social order and, less often, to understand the functions of religion in maintaining the psychological support of the individual. Terminology developing later gave the names "implicit functions" or "latent functions" to unintended and hidden effects as opposed to the name "manifest functions" or "explicit functions" for the stated or obvious goals of acts. Attempts to see the implicit functions of religion came principally through close scrutiny of the social realm, determining the social identities of the actors in ritual, the nature of their relations with other people involved and to the whole society, and the social problems the members of society faced. Every religious custom was seen to play socially supportive roles. Although disruptive effects were evident, such as the fear that is instilled by some religious beliefs and the inhibitions that supernaturalistic interpretations might place upon the growth of knowledge and economic development, these were seldom given any more than cursory attention.

Application of these guiding ideas and techniques of research resulted in many studies that are repetitious, resembling form letters. The modern tendency toward decline of this kind of functionalist study in favor of others that deal with functional relationships without explicitly relating them to human well-being or human concerns is surely in part attributable to excellence; that is, interpretations of the socially and psychologically supportive roles of religion have in general been so convincing that repetition no longer seems profitable.

A detailed blueprint of the functional significance of a rite of passage derived from the analysis of an elaborate rite in one society, for example, may often be used for rites of passage of other societies. These rites serve to give psychological support to the individual, easing him through the social transition and announcing publicly his new status, and they support social solidarity by joint action and joint expression of beliefs and values.

In the chapters that follow we shall examine in greater detail the beliefs and acts of supernaturalism that appear to be universal among human societies and the classes or categories that stand out most prominently, presenting in conclusion a summing up of the prevailing anthropological views of the nature of religion. For now, it is useful to make a brief summary of the aims, procedures, and basic assumptions discussed in the preceding pages. Anthropology has set apart one category of human behavior as supernaturalism or religion. This class of beliefs and acts is man-made and everywhere much alike. As a creation of man, religion is an element of culture, a man-made part of the human universe, which has fostered the perpetuation and increase of the human species. As a part of the system called culture, religion affects and is affected by other elements of the system, such as the social order and the manner of gaining a livelihood. The anthropological study of religion has been first a matter of collecting and classifying information on religious beliefs and practices. This step has been followed and often accompanied by attempts to account for similarities and differences. What is alike and what is different are, of course, two faces of the same coin. More than anything else, the pages which follow point to the essential identity of mankind everywhere.

2

Religious Beginnings

About a century ago, when anthropology took form as an organized scientific field, the principal subject of investigation was the manner in which culture had evolved from the very simple beginnings in antiquity that had become known from the researches of archeologists. The theory of biological evolution as set forth by Charles Darwin was then a new, exciting, and revolutionary idea in the scientific world. Analogous ideas of cultural evolution, like the antecedents of the theories of Darwin, had by this time a long history that may be traced back to philosophers of classical Greece, but they had never been an outstanding trend of intellectual thought. Stimulated by the general scientific growth of the nineteenth century and doubtless also by the intellectual excitement over the theory of biological evolution, the idea of cultural evolution then became the dominant current of theory in anthropology.

Early anthropologists interested in religion asked how it began and how it grew and changed to its evolutionary peak, which they assumed to be monotheism, the form of religion of the European societies of the scholars themselves. The prevailing view held that religion had evolved from primitive beliefs in many spiritual beings to belief in a single omnipotent being, as exemplified by the Christian God. Similarly, the early cultural evolutionists thought that marriage and the human family evolved from promiscuity (the "promiscuous horde") through various stages of polygamy on to the final form of the family based on monogamous marriage.

By the early twentieth century, these theories of the evolution of religion had been discarded as unsound, but an associated group of ideas are alive today in modified form. As integral to their ideas of evolution, nineteenth century scholars were concerned with origins. Seeing ideas and acts of supernaturalism as distinctive and everywhere remarkably similar, they speculated about the conditions—the intellectual and emotional traits of man and the nature of the world in which he lived—that might have led him to formulate ideas of supernaturalism. Edward Burnett Tylor, the most noted of the pioneer anthropologists, thought that man hit upon the idea of spiritual beings in trying to explain the difference between life and death and the things that he seemed to do in dreams and trances. To explain these things, man developed the idea of a soul separable from the body, a spiritual entity that leaves the body at death and during sleep and other states of unconsciousness. From this simple beginning, man extended the idea of animism or belief in spiritual beings to the animate and inanimate world, giving spirits or souls to living things and sometimes to inanimate objects. Other scholars of the time called Naturists saw the beginnings of religion in the emotional reactions of awe, respect, and fear that were said to have been naturally evoked in primeval man by natural phenomena, such as the sun, moon, and storms, which man then personified.

Early twentieth century theorists presented ideas of the origins of religion that are regarded as different from those of their predecessors but nevertheless share fundamental similarities. Many theorists have regarded religion as a response to fear, dissatisfaction, and insecurity. The noted French sociologist, Émile Durkheim, whose ideas have been important in the development of anthropology, saw religious symbols as the objectification of society, so that religious acts were the unconscious worship of society. Only society, Durkheim held, could evoke the attitudes that we call religious, and the joint expression of the moral sentiments of a society through religious ideology and acts was the bond that held society together. In his view, religion and society were thus inseparable and, since society was fundamentally a moral communion, essentially identical.

Making use of nineteenth century ideas of the evolution of marriage and the family, Sigmund Freud offered a theory of religious genesis that is at the same time an interpretation of the origin of the Oedipus complex. His interpretation seemingly emphasizes sexuality but in other ways it shares the traits of other theorists. According to Freud, primeval man lived in a promiscuous horde without marriage and without control of sexual behavior beyond brute strength. Primeval sons, in jealousy over the sexual monopoly of females by the patriarchal father, banded together and killed him. Ambivalently loving and hating the father, the sons in atonement began worshipping his spirit, creating God the Father.

Speculations were also made about the genesis of magic, of which the best known comes from Sir James George Frazer, writing in the early twentieth century. Frazer likened magic to science, calling magic the pseudoscience of primitive man, discarded as a means of control when man saw that it was not effective and replaced by the worship of supernatural beings, which Frazer called religion. Other anthropologists, such as the pioneer functionalist Bronislaw Malinowski, saw magic as a response to feelings of insecurity, stating that in important activities of mankind a great breach lay between naturalistic procedures aimed at goals, such as farming or fishing, and success in reaching those goals. Magic, he said, filled the breach, giving feelings of security vital for human existence.

To educated people today, most of these ideas seem strange, outmoded, unverifiable, or perhaps inconsequential. All specific interpretations have generally been rejected by modern scholars or set aside as unverifiable. It is true, for example, that all historically known societies have concepts of the human soul that leaves the body at death and, in some societies, during sleep, but no techniques are available to allow us to state with certainty that Tylor's idea of the mode of their creation is sound. Other objections to these views may also be made, of which ethnocentrism stands out. Sigmund Freud's view of the primeval creation of God the Father, for example, is congruent with the religion and familial relations of the Viennese Jewish society in which Freud lived. As we shall see, however, a concept of the father as a god is wholly incongruent for some societies and does not exist.

In one way or another these old views reflect ideas about the nature of religion and the mode of its creation that are current today. These include the roles of symbolism, projection, objectification of human emotional states, and the idea that religion is a technique for dealing with the human problems which has served man in many ways. The current modern view of religion, as stated in our Introduction, includes generalized ideas of its genesis. Religion is seen as the projection by man of his own qualities and of his experiences with the world outside himself to create the realm of supernaturalism, a process that rests upon man's unique ability to symbolize, to think abstractly, and arbitrarily to attach meanings to objects, conditions, and acts. This view may be summarized in the statement that man created god and gods in his own image. A brief worldwide survey of ideas of supernaturalism and associated practices will serve to illustrate.

The entire roster of supernatural entities may be classified under the two headings of personified and impersonal concepts of the supernatural. These concepts may readily be seen as having secular counterparts; no ideas of supernatural entities lack such mundane counterparts or analogies. The associated acts of religion may also readily be seen as congruent with views of supernatural forces. Through the ideas of supernaturalism man objectifies and thereby makes comprehensible his wishes, fears, ideals, dislikes, and disappointments; his objectifications suggest and perhaps compel courses of action that we call religious or supernaturalistic.

PERSONIFIED CONCEPTS AND ASSOCIATED ACTS

All supernatural beings—that is, supernatural entities with the quality of life—share with man certain important and unique qualities and all have traits and capabilities that have meaning to the members of the societies which have created or accepted them. Gods of war find no place in the pantheons of great modern nations, and the mortality rate of gods of agriculture has been high in the last century. God as a father finds no place in societies in which the social role of the father with respect to his children is economically, socially, and psychologically unimportant, where, as in a number of tribal societies that trace their descent matrilineally, through female lines, the economic provider and adult male socializer of children is the mother's brother. God the Nephew is a concept compatible in aboriginal times with the social organization and other conditions of life of the Fox Indians of the midwestern United States. To the male Fox Indian the most important supernatural being was his individual guardian spirit, whom he addressed as "nephew." In Fox society, the relationship of uncle and nephew was important, a relationship of intimacy, equality, and mutual helpfulness.

The range of supernatural beings is large, extending from souls and spirits to great and powerful gods. Some are concretely conceived as having the forms of human males and females, lower animals, or natural phenomena. Others are abstract or vaguely conceived entities lacking bodily form, such as "Space," "Whiteness," and human moral qualities. Although only a part of the gods are anthropomorphic, having the bodily form of man, all share traits that are necessary for comprehension by and communication with human beings. In the word of William Goode (1951: 43), all are *anthropopsychic*, having the psyches or personalities of man. Regardless of their forms, anthropomorphic, zoomorphic, vague, or invisible, the international roster of spiritual beings coincides with a pan-human inventory of the traits of personality and character of man, their creator. They understand man and his culture and can communicate with him, if sometimes in mysterious ways. They have ideals, hopes, wishes, fears, and feel anger and frustration. They are kind, loving, stern; they may judge and give rewards and punishments. Like some men, spiritual beings occasionally may be deceitful, cruel, jealous, harmful, and have other base traits of man. Some beings are eternally good and others, the objectifications of fears and hatreds, eternally malevolent and immoral. Like man, gods may be alternately good and bad, wise and foolish, and temperate and intemperate. Scholars of religion long ago gave the name Trickster Gods to beings of this kind who, like the Norse god Loki, the god Susanowo-No-Mikoto of ancient Japanese Shinto, and numerous gods of primitive societies, are alternately good and bad. The Christian God is eternally good but traditional Christianity provides in the Devil a concentration of all the evil qualities of mankind. The Devil, we may note, is unsuitable to most of us today as an explanation for immoral or otherwise undesirable behavior. He has accordingly joined the large international list of moribund supernatural beings, and remains alive for many of us only as an unconscious echo in our expressions, "I don't know what possessed me" and "I don't know what got into me."

One difference between gods and man stands out and is implied by the word "supernaturalistic." Supernatural beings tend strongly to exceed the natural or normal for living man; they are generally more understanding, more powerful, more virtuous, and more wicked than man, and they usually have all other human capabilities and traits of personality and character in intensified degree.

Religious behavior toward supernatural beings accords with their qualities; that is, man acts toward them quite as he acts toward other men, good and evil. Most human relations are cordial, hospitable, friendly, and considerate of fellow men. When human beings have authority over others or hold eminence otherwise derived, they are accorded respect by their fellow men. Most of the institutionalized human ways of communicating with supernatural beings are similarly hospitable acts that seek to please, honor, and win favor of beings that somehow stand in superior positions. What is pleasing to man is pleasing to gods, who respond favorably to gifts, sacrifices, acts of reverence, eulogies, and, where gods are moral guardians, to records of virtuous behavior. As among many North American Indian societies before the arrival of Europeans, man might also seek the aid of gods by evoking feelings of pity, calling attention to his miserable condition. Where conceptions of gods are extremely anthropomorphic, behavior toward them reaches heights of anthropocentrism. A main task of ancient Egyptian priests was to care for the gods as if they were human, awakening them—that is, their statues—bathing and feeding them, and putting them to bed at night. The foundress of the Tenrikyo sect of modern Japan, a peasant woman of the eighteenth century who claimed divinity, is similarly treated today. Three times daily her spirit is served meals in a special hall at the headquarters of the sect.

Pleasing behavior extended to the gods has many forms and sometimes includes entertainment. In various aboriginal kingdoms of Africa the powerful spirits of deceased kings were honored at fixed times by storytelling and other forms of pleasurable entertainment.

All human behavior is not pleasing or hospitable, of course. Like evil men, harmful supernatural beings are disliked and feared. Like human enemies, one must protect oneself from evil spirits and gods, and one may think it necessary to attack them. Since most benevolent gods are powerful and wise, behavior toward them is generally deferential and honest, but, as in some Melanesian societies, the gods may be deceived by empty promises.

Gods and spirits who are not regarded as evil sometimes fail to respond to human requests. When repeated hospitable behavior fails to bring results, the standardized practice may be coercion. Gods may be reviled, threatened, or physically punished in symbolic ways. Eskimo gods of the wind and weather who, after repeated entreaties, failed to bring calm seas were punished by stabbing the wind with a knife and lashing the surface of the sea with a dog whip. Customs of punishing tutelary gods and saints who failed to answer pleas for rain were formerly widespread in Asia and Europe. Statues of saints and tutelary gods were turned in the wrong direction, left on their backs in the hot sun, or subjected to indignities such as being fettered by ropes or having their garments damaged.

IMPERSONAL CONCEPTS AND ASSOCIATED ACTS

To people reared in the Judeo-Christian tradition, impersonal concepts of supernatural power are generally unfamiliar. Magic is an exception that is known if not practiced by all, but Judeo-Christian belief ideally excludes magic. Judaism, Christianity, and Islam, historically related and fundamentally similar religions, may all be described as strongly emphasizing personified concepts of the supernatural, but each includes some ideas of impersonal supernatural power. A mixture of the two ideas is, in fact, characteristic of religious complexes everywhere, a mixture in which one or the other conception may dominate or in which both concepts intermingle in ways that make them seem of equal importance.

In the course of his ordinary life as a social animal, man has much contact with his fellow man. His experiences also bring him constantly into contact with the world outside himself and other members of his species. He understands the qualities and capabilities of himself and other human beings. He also understands in ways that make life possible for him the entire outside universe, much of which is inanimate. Inanimate objects have qualities known to him; they are soft or hard, sweet or sour, hot or cold, sharp or dull, poisonous or edible, harmful or unharmful. He also knows that certain acts such as cooking foods, firing clay to make pottery, planting seeds of grain, and shooting or being shot with an arrow lead to desired and undesired results. On a supernatural level, he has created ideas of substantival, objectlike power that may be seen as analogous with the properties of objects and substances lacking the vital essence or the quality of life, and of power or efficiency analogous with the effects of mundane acts. Impersonal supernatural power, unlike supernatural beings, is not sentient, does not have hopes, wishes, and fears and does not see, hear, feel, or think.

As a conception of power existing everywhere in the universe or inhering in certain objects and acts, impersonal power is the inanimate counterpart of supernatural beings. It works most frequently to the benefit of man but is often harmful. It may be wholly beneficial to all human beings, harmful to some, or harmful to all. Accordingly, a vast collection of procedures have developed for gaining, controlling, using, and protecting oneself against the qualities or effects of such power.

In modern Christianity such conceptions of power are relatively rare. Power inheres in the Cross, holy water, talismans such as St. Christopher's medals, in the acts of the sacrament of Communion, and, of waning importance, in the relics of saints and other objects. This power is generally thought to have been bestowed by supernatural beings, but, once granted, it becomes an inanimate substance. In Western folk belief many objects and acts similarly have extra-natural power, such as the rabbit's foot, the number 13, and casting salt over one's shoulder. Elsewhere in the world, ideas of impersonal power are abundant and often complex, some-times intimately associated with supernatural beings and often quite independent of them. Gods may confer the power upon human beings, who may then make use of it. In some societies this is done only with the aid of the gods and in others independently of them, treating the power as if it were a commodity. Power may flow and be transmitted by physical contact or in other ways. In some societies, such as various American Indian tribes of the Great Plains, power might be sold, given away, or inherited.

Like the gods, impersonal power might be omnipotent, useful for success in all things, or it might be highly specialized. Among Indian societies of far western North America, power came in many specialized forms, such as doctoring power, snake power that made its possessor immune to the poison of rattlesnakes, love power, power to charm antelopes—that is, to attract them so that they might be shot—and power to perform witchcraft.

As a mysterious substance or force, impersonal power is seldom given concrete form and is generally invisible and intangible. Some distinctive physical trait, such as a white forelock, might indicate that a person possesses such power, and, now and then, specialized kinds of power are concretely visualized. Among the Tiv of Nigeria, for example, witchcraft power was a black, fatty substance around the heart of people who were witches.

In many societies, the holding and use of impersonal power have been the key to success, and the successful are assumed to control an extraordinary amount of power. In anthropological writings, the best-known examples of such power are the *mana* of aboriginal Melanesia and Polynesia and concepts of power, variously named, of North American Indian societies. In Melanesia, mana existed everywhere in the universe and worked for both good and bad. In keeping with the egalitarian social order of Melanesia, techniques for amassing mana were equally available to all. In Polynesia, where social classes of aristocrats and commoners existed, mana was also everywhere and techniques were available for gaining it, but the amount of mana one possessed also accorded inherently with one's social status. All people had some mana, but kings and aristocrats inherently had much more than commoners. Since mana flowed like electricity, it was dangerous to commoners, who were unsuited for containing or conducting large quantities. To prevent sick-ness or death from an overcharge of mana, elaborate rules—taboos—governed the relations between nobles and commoners. Wherever the king of Hawaii trod and where his shadow fell became dangerous ground, charged with mana. In traveling, the royal family of Hawaii was transported on the shoulders of relay teams of specially insulated porters, making the transfer from one bearer to another by leaping from one set of shoulders to another without touching the ground.

In many North American Indian societies, success in life was thought to depend upon the acquisition of power, gained individually through a vision or revelation.

Revelations as the source of power came in some societies through dreams and in others were actively sought by established procedures. Isolating himself from others, the seeker gazed at the sun, went without food and water, pierced his flesh, and practiced other forms of self-torture to produce a hallucinatory revelation that indicated the acquisition of power. Fortified by the revelation and the knowledge that he now possessed power, the seeker returned to his group full of confidence in his future success.

Following the spread of European culture to the rest of the world and the growth of scientific interpretations, many ideas and practices relating to impersonal power have become uncommon or extinct. Certain kinds of magical practices that will later be discussed remain common everywhere, however, and one conception of substantival impersonal power existing in the past if not today in the beliefs of every society is still far from dead. This is the idea of harmful pollution that inheres in death and blood, especially in human females, who menstruate and who pass blood during childbirth. Special prescriptions and proscriptions on the behavior of women that relate to pollution are alive today in many societies, primitive and non-primitive. The idea of *marhime*, the polluting influence of women and an associated complex of taboos, is alive among modern gypsies, and similar ideas disappeared only in recent centuries from European countries. Orthodox Judaism retains vestiges of former beliefs and practices of this kind. The core of traditional Japanese Shinto rested on ideas of pollution and purification, and some practices restricting the behavior of women continue to have life in Japan. For example, during menstrual periods and for a time after childbirth women should not visit Shinto shrines or have any other contact with supernatural beings of the Shinto pantheon. Concepts of pollution remain strong in India, where they extend beyond the baleful influence of women to social statuses of caste and may be seen to serve as a rationale for the hierarchy of castes. A modern account of India states:

> Pollution is contagious. Always transferable by physical contact, it can sometimes radiate out from a source and pollute even without actual contact. Birth and death, for example, radiate pollution along the lines of kinship. Close agnatic kin are polluted by deaths and births occurring even outside their immediate families and must undergo seclusion and purification ritual. Sexual relations render the participants impure, and abstinence from sex is prescribed before important rituals. Sexual relations between persons of unequal rank are highly polluting for the higher ranked partner, particularly if female. Defilement can be so severe that there can be no recovery, and the woman must be evicted from her caste before her pollution contaminates everyone else. Permanent pollution, too, is contagious within a whole caste group. Barbers are polluted because they come in contact with the polluted hair trimmings of their clients and even though one may never have cut hair or given another person a shave, the fact of being born into the Barber caste transmits the impurity of all Barbers to oneself.
>
> The hierarchy of relative pollution includes most things in the universe. Species of animals and plants, earth, fire, air, water, even the gods fall within the range. . . . Times of danger—an eclipse, a new- or full-moon day—are times of danger requiring special precautions against pollution. All things have an inherent degree of pollution, some things being inherently more polluted than others. Purity too, is inherent and some things are inherently more pure than others. Running water is pure and the morning bath in water flowing over one's head is a major aspect of all purificatory rites. Cleansing must be done to the accompaniment of ritual gestures and words. Other purifying agents include

fire, the sun, earth, Sanskrit characters, and especially water from the Ganges. The products of the cow have great purifying power, and the most potent purifying potion is a mixture of the five products of the cow . . . milk, curds, ghi (clarified butter), dung, and urine (Tyler 1973:79–80).

BEHAVIOR ASSOCIATED WITH IMPERSONAL POWER

Most of the beliefs in impersonal power and acts associated with them are ordinarily labeled as magic. Except in moments of emotional stress, such as when one kicks a door that fails to operate properly, man does not use the behavior of interpersonal human relations in dealing with objects and substances. Instead, he manipulates them mechanically. By common definition, magic is also mechanical manipulation or implies special substantival power. Like other kinds of super-naturalistic behavior, the ideas and procedures of magic are everywhere similar and may be classified under the headings of imitative magic, contagious magic, sequential magic, and divination. In addition, many objects have inherent super-natural powers. If these are protective or helpful we often call them *talismans* (and when that power is conceived in personified form, as the property of an indwelling spiritual being, the usual term is *fetish*). No generic term name exists for the entire group of objects credited with impersonal power. The range is huge, including numbers, words, and other man-made symbols, as well as natural objects. It is clear that man can attribute supernatural significance to any kind of object, substance, or act.

One distinctive group of entities with supernatural significance is called *totems*. Totemic beliefs and practices are widespread and variable, but all have a central idea of mystic affinity between the members of a social group and their totem, which is most frequently an animal—frequently an animal of economic importance to them, such as the kangaroo, wallaby, and witchetty grub totems of Australian aborigines— but sometimes a plant or occasionally some inanimate natural phenomenon. Societies with totems frequently regard themselves as being descendants of their totems. In their importance as symbols of social identification, totems are essen-tially the supernatural counterparts of flags and similar secular symbols of social or national identity. In some primitive societies, such as those of the native inhabitants of Australia, beliefs of totemism and associated rites have been the outstanding feature of religion. Noting the importance of totemism to Australian aborigines and regarding their extremely simple culture as representative of the condition of life of primeval man, Émile Durkheim once advanced the idea that totemism was the first form of religion, an interpretation in keeping with his ideas of the intimate link between society and religion.

Most of the acts of magic reflect ideas of sympathy or connection, sometimes mysterious and sometimes evident. The worldwide similarity in the seeming philosophic basis in acts of magic was noted long ago by Frazer (1928:11), who described them as operating according to two "principles of thought," the Law of Similarity (like produces like) and the Law of Contact or Contagion (the belief that things once in association remain forever in association). Imitative magic tries to reach its goals by simulating them in such acts as symbolically depicting rain, pregnancy, successful childbirth, or the production of bountiful crops. Contagious magic is exemplified by numerous practices of performing acts upon hair combings, nail clippings, and articles of clothing with the belief that the acts affect the people from whom they came. Like the foregoing examples, much magic combines the principles of similarity and contact.

The idea of sympathy or connection also applies to sequential magic, but the connection is often one of invisible strings: Event B automatically follows the performance of event A, sometimes beneficially and sometimes harmfully. Performing a specified ritual act four times, for example, may bring desired results, and walking beneath a ladder brings calamity.

Among the common forms of magic, divination stands apart in being supernatural vision or judgment that seeks knowledge rather than control. The forms and specific acts of divination are beyond counting and are often bizarre. An ancient Inca practice sought divinatory answers by use of a spider which was placed on a hoop of tightly stretched fabric. The rim of the hoop was struck forcibly and repeatedly until a leg of the spider fell off; divination was then made on the basis of the position of the severed leg. Particularly widespread forms of divination include the observation of the flight of birds, examination of the liver and other internal organs of animals, and astrology.

Divination by ordeal has a long history in Europe, Africa, and various societies elsewhere as a form of evidence in cases of law. African societies often used poisons, sometimes given to chickens rather than to the people accused of offenses. Ordeals by hot iron and by casting the accused in water were used in Europe until recent centuries. As our Introduction notes, these ordeals often appear to give the accused no chance of survival. They nevertheless have an ancient history of survival in many societies and therefore of presumed social success. A number of conditioning circumstances seem to offer an explanation. One is that diviners appear to make their judgments to accord with public opinion, and public opinion usually held that the accused was guilty. When public opinion is against the accused, he becomes a source of social disruption until or unless he is punished even if he is innocent. Divination may also be seen as socially advantageous by removing from human beings the onus, and possible stigma, of making judgment of guilt or innocence and laying the responsibility on supernatural beings or forces.

Among the forms of magic, divination also stands out in being by far the most robust survivor in the modern world. Its special appeal is personal. Scientific prediction tells us many things of importance in our personal lives but the expectations it predicts are modes or means. Only divination tells the individual what will happen to him as an individual.

The preceding account of concepts and acts of supernaturalism has made a sharp distinction between the personified and impersonal. These ideas and acts are philosophically distinguishable and, like the Western concepts of magic and religion, often stand apart in the minds of their performers, but in no society does one set exist alone. In elaborate rituals both are commonly intermingled. Mechanical acts of magic may accompany prayer and sacrifice, and acts of magic may compel spiritual beings to act in accord with the wishes of the human performers. As we have noted, impersonal power may be conferred by spiritual beings. Among supernatural beings, power may flow, growing and declining as the result of acts of rivalry among those beings. Very often, the two sets of ideas are inextricably mixed. In the anthropological view, both sets hold much in common, especially in their significance in human life, and, as we have noted, anthropological interpretation of their significance has scarcely distinguished them.

Our account in the foregoing pages has also inferentially presented an interpretation of the origins of religion as a projective creation of man that reflects himself and the world of his experience. From the more direct evidence of archeology, we may infer with considerable assurance that ideas and practices of supernaturalism are ancient. We may see also that if the archeological interpretation is sound, the earliest forms of supernaturalism are thoroughly familiar, having many historic and modern counterparts.

The earliest suggestions or evidence of the existence of supernaturalism are found in association with the remains of Neanderthal man in various sites in Europe and southwest Asia, perhaps as many as 60,000 years ago. Neanderthal man carefully buried his dead and placed in the graves with them stone tools, practices which are thought to indicate belief in an afterlife in which the spirits of the objects placed in the grave accompany the spirits of the deceased to another world. In one recently discovered burial in Iraq, the deceased was interred with hundreds of flower blossoms. Neanderthal man may also have had cult beliefs centering on cave bears, since excavation of a number of Neanderthal sites in Europe has revealed collections, sometimes arranged symmetrically, of the skulls of the bears.

During the late Stone Age of Europe, evidence of the existence of man himself and of supernaturalism are much more abundant. Cro-Magnon man of about thirty to ten thousand years ago, indistinguishable in physical traits from modern man, also buried his dead accompanied by grave goods and decorated with red ochre. He was, moreover, an artist, whose paintings in caves and other forms of art include many works that must have had supernatural goals. Paintings with mineral pigments are the most abundant, but other less common forms of art were sculpture in the round, carvings on bone and antler, and the modeling of figures in clay. Evidence of supernaturalism comes in part from the motifs of much of the art. Animals are often depicted in paintings as wounded by spears or dying, which is seen to be imitative magic, and a few paintings appear to show primitive priests conducting rites. Other traits of the paintings also suggest supernaturalistic intent. Many were painted in the dark inner recesses of caves, places that are difficult to reach and where artificial illumination by means of stone lamps burning animal fats was necessary. At one site, the paintings are about a mile from the cave entrance in a gallery that can be reached only by passing through a siphon in an underground stream. Small sculptures in sandstone and ivory called Paleolithic "Venuses" depict seemingly pregnant women, and carvings of bone and antler similarly sometimes appear to be examples of imitative magic, depicting pregnant animals. Like the skulls of cave bears found at Neanderthal sites, the relatively few modelings in clay found on the floors of caves once occupied by Cro-Magnon man strongly suggest cults or magic rites centered on cave bears and other dangerous animals. Archeological excavations of sites of later human occupation have revealed many Venuses and much more evidence of beliefs of supernaturalism that appear to correspond closely with historic and modern circumstances. It seems safe to assume that supernaturalism is old, perhaps as old as man.

PART II

The Roles of Religion in Human Life

3
Introduction

Educated citizens of the culturally advanced societies of the world have long been scientifically sophisticated in looking at the conditions of their own lives; that is, they have learned and express views of the nature of social life and culture that accord with or derive from the physical and, especially, the social sciences. The educated public no longer regards crime, juvenile delinquency, student riots, sexual deviancy, and alcoholism as the independently willful acts of morally reprehensible people individually responsible for their wrongdoing. These are instead regarded as defections stemming from certain sociocultural circumstances, the correction of which should consist of remedial social changes.

Similar sophistication also often extends to interpretations of the roles of religion in human life. Without personally holding religious faith—which puts the role of religion into quite a different cast—the modern citizen is aware of the role of religious views and creeds in explaining the universe, providing comfort, solace, and hope to individuals, thereby also contributing to social harmony, and as a moral force that has value to both the individual and his society. These are all views and interpretations which anthropology also offers, elaborates, and, in some measure modifies on the basis of comparative information drawn from many societies rather than only the Western world. The chapters that follow reflect these current views of religion, presenting them on a comparative crosscultural background and qualifying or otherwise modifying them. Such qualifications and modifications are based upon comparative information. The views of educated citizens are seldom so based, resting instead upon unwitting ethnocentric observation of the circumstances in their own societies.

Statements made in our introductory chapter embrace in a generalized way most of the range of the roles in human life that anthropology attributes to religion— as explanatory, and in many ways psychologically reassuring, and as socially supportive by providing validations for existence, motives for human action, and as a sanction for orderly human relations. Our introductory statements have also directly and indirectly referred to negative effects of religion, such as instilling fear (which prescribed religious behavior also allays) and the seemingly disruptive effects of various religious beliefs and acts. These also will be discussed.

Religion, like all other cultural behavior, operates through the thoughts and acts of individual human beings. Its roles thus apply to individuals, and, since individuals are members of society, through them to affect social groups. Modern life in the United States has stressed individualism, and many writings by clergymen and religiously-minded sociologists have accordingly stressed the importance of religion —that is, of Christianity—as a personal or individual faith which is personally and individually rewarding. This view reflects a trend of modern life as well as modern thought but it cannot reasonably be extended to religion in a generic sense. At least, it has not been the practice of anthropology to do so. Religious beliefs and acts are not the unique, wholly independent creations of individuals but are items of culture that are learned, transmitted to others, and modified, essentially unconsciously, in accord with changes that occur in life. Religious uniqueness among the people of any society may be seen as a matter of variation in detail. Even religious reformers, who perhaps characteristically see themselves as uniquely different, are elements of a mode, a current of change arising from changes in conditions of life. It is, of course, individual people who create culture and transmit it to others, but the religious reformer could have no existence except as part of a social group, pattern, or modality.

The descriptions and discussions that follow will sometimes deal directly with the role of religion in the life of the individual. More frequently they will concern society or social groups and the relationships of religious beliefs and acts to social structure and other elements of culture. This procedure seems appropriate since the role of religion for the individual may readily be inferred when it is not stated. It is appropriate also in reflecting the dominant trend of study in anthropology, a concern with groups and modes rather than with individuals and the behavior of individuals, and a concern with culture as a system studied apart from individual people.

The myriad views and acts of religion existing among the thousands of historically known societies of the world cannot, of course, be discussed in these few chapters. Some subjects, such as myths and the traits of medicine men, shamans, seers, prophets, priests, and other specialists in religion, will have brief mention only in passing. Topics given more detailed discussion have been selected principally because they represent major subjects of anthropological study, past or present, and should, therefore, give the reader an overall view of the nature of religious thought and act throughout the world as well as of prevailing anthropological trends in the interpretation of them. Some subjects dealt with here are old and are given no intense scholarly attention today; others are topics of current investigations; and still others are on the horizon.

4

Manners, Morals, and Supernatural Sanctions

Residents of the Western world tend strongly to identify religion with morality, seeing as the greatest strength of religion its force as a sanction for moral behavior and sometimes defining religion as a moral code. Perhaps few people think today that moral codes are supported only by religion, but the relationship between religion and morality is nevertheless generally regarded as intimate, and no one has difficulty in understanding such idiomatic expressions as "more Christian than a Christian."

A look at circumstances elsewhere in the world quickly reveals this view as an ethnocentric projection based on knowledge limited to the Judeo-Christian tradition, in which religion and morality have indeed been closely associated. The question of the nature of the relationship between religion and morality was examined in the infancy of anthropology by Edward Burnett Tylor, who, on the basis of information drawn from many societies, presented a conclusion that has since often been elaborated by later anthropologists but has never been fundamentally changed: No necessary or inherent relationship exists. Religion and morality are distinguishable categories of ideas and acts that may exist independently of each other or in any degree of association from remote to a condition of intimacy that can be called identity.

Information supporting this conclusion available on foreign societies in 1871, the date of Tylor's publication, was fairly abundant and it has since grown vastly. Moral codes—ideals of the proper behavior of man toward man—exist in all societies and are necessary for the survival of society and the human species. Like religious beliefs, moral rules differ from society to society as other features of the cultures differ, but all have a common core as ideas of propriety in human relations that makes life tenable. Moral codes define privileges and obligations and prescribe and proscribe courses of action for members of society. Anthropologists assume, in fact, that moral codes are as old as man is old, that their formulation has been part of the complex of self-domestication that fostered the evolutionary emergence of *Homo sapiens* from earlier primates which lacked religion, morality, and other attributes of culture.

All societies have moral codes and all have conventionalized means of supporting them. Social sanctions, forms of approval and disapproval of behavior, are everywhere much alike. Uniqueness is primarily a matter of emphasis upon certain kinds of sanctions and the weakness of other sanctions. Only occasionally is any distinctive type of sanction totally absent. No thorough or comprehensive scheme of classification of social sanctions has ever been formulated, although the sanctioning force of many acts and attitudes has often been noted. For the most part, sanctions are known by their names in everyday vocabularies: praise and rewards of many other kinds, loss or gain of social prestige, ridicule, avoidance, ostracism, physical punishment, legal sanctions, and supernatural rewards and punishments. In any society, many of the moral rules tend strongly to become cherished ideals that are looked upon as eternal verities, and observing them becomes an end in itself. The sanctions also tend to become internalized so that actual exercise of them is unnecessary and conscience serves as the monitor. When rules of behavior regarded as extremely important are violated, an intense concentration of sanctions is characteristically imposed. Characteristically also, greatest emphasis is given to the moral rules which seem in greatest danger of violation, and the sanctions for these rules are stressed.

Probably every society has a few supernatural sanctions for specific infractions of moral rules. Automatic and impersonal misfortune of a supernatural kind or punishment by a spiritual being are common sanctions for incest. But in many societies morality and religion touch upon each other only here and there, and moral ideals of the greatest importance may have no supernatural sanctions. One's conduct in life may have no bearing on the fate of the soul after death, which might be the same for the virtuous and the wicked or depend upon one's age, sex, occupation, social status, manner of death, or kind of funeral service. Whereas ideas of impersonal power are important, morality tends to be remote from supernaturalism, but even in such societies certain offenses may inexorably bring grave misfortune. Many other illustrations of the lack of association or weak association of religion and morality may be drawn from information on primitive societies but illustrations are available closer at hand. For example, we have no reason to accuse of immorality, as we have defined it, the many nonreligious citizens of modern Japan, where only about 30 percent of the population declares itself as affiliated with any religious sect.

None of the foregoing words are to deny that religion may have moral import. In some primitive societies as well as in culturally advanced societies, it is a strong force for moral rectitude. Its force is not limited to direct supernatural sanctions but may, in a variety of ways and degrees, operate indirectly, although some of these ways may strain Western conceptions of morality. For example, supernatural sanctions for immorality may be seen as extraordinarily powerful in societies in which infractions bring punishment to any member of the group, thus frequently failing to strike the offender. As a result everyone then becomes the monitor for the behavior of everyone else. In the many societies of the past where rulers were regarded as divine or semidivine and the welfare of the society was thought to be intimately linked with the acts and welfare of the ruler, royal mandates became religious rules and violation of them was a sin. Ancestor worship, or reverence for ancestral spirits, may also sanction morality in either a specific or generalized way. In the Melanesian society of the Manus, the stern spirit of the most recently deceased male head of the household observed the moral behavior of his living relatives much like the fundamentalist conception of God, giving rewards and punishments. In various sub-Saharan societies of Africa ancestral spirits acted similarly. In other African societies and in China and Japan, ancestral spirits sanctioned behavior less directly. They were honored in ritual and in behavior, and immoral conduct offended them or besmirched their memories.

WITCHCRAFT AND SORCERY

Supernatural sanctions for moral behavior, as we have seen, are not limited to the acts of gods or other sentient supernatural beings. Beliefs and practices of witchcraft and sorcery may also be seen to have these as well as other individually and socially supportive effects. The terms witchcraft and sorcery are used by anthropologists to distinguish different kinds of supernaturalistic ideas and acts, both of which may be found in a single society and frequently coexisted in societies of black Africa. Witchcraft implies that the actor, the witch, is inherently harmful, sometimes inherently immoral. Without performing any physical act of hostility, the witch in many societies may harm others simply by wishing, thinking, or even unconsciously projecting evil. Among the Paiute Indians of Oregon even dreaming of hostile actions toward others was witchcraft. The sorcerer is not innately evil but reaches his goals of harming or aiding others by use of the mechanical procedures ordinarily called magic.

Functional interpretations of witchcraft and sorcery are much alike. Both are seen to be institutionalized channels for the expression of hostility when other channels for resolving conflicts and releasing psychological tensions are unavailable or excessively disruptive to the society and the individual. As such, they are safety valves for the individual and are accordingly useful socially. These beliefs and practices are also seen as sanctions for moral behavior. Those who do not conform with social rules or arouse hostility for any other reason are in danger of either becoming the targets of witchcraft or else of being accused of practicing witchcraft and being subjected to temporal punishment as a witch. Accusations of witchcraft are not random but may be seen to follow patterns that reflect stressful relations between the accuser and the accused. Among the many accusations of witchcraft recorded among the Navaho, for example, the most common are those made by women accusing their fathers-in-law, with whom social relations are difficult.

Studies of witchcraft in African societies have reported its spread to societies formerly lacking witchcraft and increases in its incidence (that is, increases in the number of accusations of witchcraft) among other societies. These events have been interpreted as the result of increased social and personal stress arising from the disturbance of native ways of life through contact with European cultures under conditions which do not easily tolerate forms of aggressive hostility other than witchcraft. In these interpretations, it is manifestly the social scene—particularly the stressful relations among relatives and other persons that social schemes produce and the institutionalized and informal social mechanisms other than witchcraft which exist for solving conflicts—that is used as the key to understanding. Moral implications in these events are complex, but they are unquestionably present.

RELIGION AND ETIQUETTE

The role of supernaturalistic beliefs as a sanction for behavior reaches beyond the shadowy borders of morality into the realm of etiquette. As the anthropologist Leslie A. White has observed, the subject of etiquette has received almost no attention from the social sciences. White (1959:225–226) makes a clear distinction between etiquette and morality, stating:

> Among the parts of which every social system consists are ... *classes*. A class, as we have defined the term, is one of an indefinite number of parts of a social whole, each of which differs from the other in composition and functions. Men, women, adults, children, married, widowed, divorced, etc., are thus classes. As we have just noted above, each class must maintain its own integrity, and each one must be articulated with the others if the social system as a whole is to function harmoniously and effectively. The means of accomplishing this is a code of rules that we call *etiquette*. A code of etiquette defines each class in terms of behavior and obliges each individual to conform to the code proper to his class. In this way the identity of each class is established and its integrity maintained. Furthermore, the behavior of an individual member of a class, as prescribed by the code of etiquette, serves not only to identify him with his own class but to prescribe the proper form of social intercourse with individuals in other classes.

Restating White's ideas briefly and comparing etiquette with morality, we may say that etiquette consists of particularistic rules of behavior that apply among specific categories of people whereas moral rules are universal standards of conduct that apply to all people. In our society, a breach of etiquette must ordinarily be observed by others to become effectively a breach, but a moral failing may bring severe supernatural penalty while remaining unknown to anyone except the person who has broken the rules. In solitude, one may pick one's nose, belch, and do similar things with perfect composure.

In congruence with the traditional Western view of intimate linkage between religion and morality, members of our society characteristically look upon violations of rules of etiquette as much less serious than moral offenses. But the border between etiquette and morality is not always clear and in some foreign societies rules that we call etiquette take on the hue of morality and are supernaturally sanctioned. The beliefs and practices of mana and taboo of aboriginal Polynesia are a striking example. Many of the taboos were particularistic, defining courses of action of classes of people in relation to other classes, and these were the most powerful taboos. Women, who held lower social positions than men, were prohibited from eating certain foods and denied other privileges open to men. The very strictest taboos applied to the relations between commoners and royalty, and violation of these customs brought death from an overcharge of mana. Commoners could ordinarily have no direct contact with royalty, walk where royal feet had set, or, in the presence of royalty stand so that their bodies were above those of the rulers. Sanctions for breaking these rules were effective; even unwitting breaches could bring sickness or death once brought to the awareness of the offender. As with witchcraft and other forms of black magic, taboos operate by internalization or magical fright. To become sick or die, the violator of a taboo and the victim of harmful magic need only know or think that he has violated a taboo or that magic has been worked against him. The role of Polynesian ideas of mana and taboo in supporting the social hierarchy is easy to see.

In historic Japan, etiquette also took on the appearance of morality. Under the feudal regime that endured in Japan for centuries until about one hundred years ago, society was rigidly hierarchical. Universalistic rules of morality existed, of course, but, as far as the record goes, these received or needed no great stress. In the Japanese view, man is naturally or innately moral, although he may stray from the natural path of moral human behavior. Both traditional Shinto and Buddhism included moral teachings, but these do not stand out as central themes of the religions. Heaviest emphasis in teachings of morality were laid upon loyalty and obligations to one's fellow men, and these ideas of propriety were clearly defined according to the classes of society. Elaborate rules of behavior applied to relations between members of all social classes, hierarchical and nonhierarchical. Greatest stress was placed upon obligations and deference upward, to people who stood in superior positions. The great virtue of the class of *samurai*, the Japanese equivalent of European knights, was loyalty to their lords, explicitly defined by ideal and act. The great virtue of any citizen was filial piety, devotion to one's parents. Relations between husband and wife and subject and ruler were also similarly idealized. Certain Buddhist and Shinto teachings came to incorporate these ideals, but their main religious support came through promulgating these ideals as the hallowed thought of the Chinese sage Confucius, and this support might best be described as quasi-religious. In Japan, Confucianism was never an organized religion that included priests, temples, parishioners, and acts of devotion. Instead certain Confucian ideals that suited the Japanese social scene were adopted—and given special authority as the wisdom of a great sage. Sanctions for conformance with the ideals were seldom supernatural. They were instead secular and operated largely by internalization although the external sanctions of scorn and contempt were powerful. Other external sanctions also applied. Sumptuary laws governed clothing, housing, and the like, denying or allowing certain goods and privileges according to social class; and a samurai might lawfully decapitate with his sword a commoner who failed to observe the etiquette of respect toward him as a representative of a superior social class.

In modern Japan, where the old social hierarchy has crumbled, these ideals and the behavior associated with them are today extinct or weakly lingering echoes. Morality is explicitly taught in the public schools and scarcely touches upon these particularistic ideals. Wholly secular, the public school teachings also conform in another way with trends of social and cultural change in Japan during the past century. The emphasis in these teachings is upon universalistic rules, one's behavior to all other people, concepts which the Japanese curiously call "public morality" and, referring to proper behavior in the commuter trains, subways, and street buses in which modern Japanese must spend much of their waking time, "transportation morality."

Since our definition of etiquette refers to distinguishable classes and categories of people, we might wonder about the existence of etiquette in egalitarian, primitive societies, where social classes do not exist and the division of labor is simple, depending upon sex and age. It is true that rules of etiquette are most elaborate and most forcibly sanctioned in culturally elaborate societies with strongly hierarchical social classes and elaborate specialization in labor. In primitive society, however, one mode of classifying people may be extremely elaborate and is customarily more complex than in the great nations of the modern world. Primitive society is organized primarily on the basis of kinship, through which all the necessities of life are obtained. Kinship is of vital importance, and the bonds between kin are correspondingly strong. It is not surprising then that rules of behavior in some primitive societies merge and sanction in identical ways behavior that our society distinguishes in the two categories of etiquette and morality. The universe of man in primitive society is in some ways very small and it includes most prominently one's kin. Impoliteness to one's relatives might bring a supernatural punishment as severe as that for theft or other offenses we regard as outright moral breaches. It is not difficult to see the social value in these societies of the ideals applying to relations of kinship and of the sanctions for these ideals.

RELIGION AND ACHIEVEMENT

Conceptions of morality have many forms and in the Western world one traditional view of morality with some historic depth is distinctive in its intensity and in its relationship to religion. The moral value in question is the "Protestant ethic," so named in the early twentieth century by the German sociologist Max Weber. The role of religion in stimulating economic development has been discussed and debated for many years since the publication of his work *The Protestant Ethic and the Spirit of Capitalism.* Weber's thesis was an argument against earlier interpretations of economic development that emphasized rational motives of human beings in economic activities and ignored expressive or emotional motives. He saw certain emotionally charged values as important in the development of capitalistic enterprise among the Protestant bourgeoisie of western European nations. As described by Weber, the Protestant ethic was an ascetic devotion to work fortified by the doctrine of vocations, which interpreted secular occupations in the same light as the call to the pulpit. Unremitting industry, thrift, frugality, and sobriety were virtues, and laziness, extravagance, and self-indulgence were sins.

Argument has since waged about the validity of Weber's interpretation, but modern scholars are in agreement in regarding the will to achieve, accompanied by restraints such as those embodied in the Protestant ethic, as fostering economic development. Weber's study has had great heuristic value, stimulating investigations of the implicit roles of religion and the general subject of motivation toward achievement. These investigations have made clear that great differences exist in attitudes toward work and achievement among societies of the world and among social classes within societies, some valuing work for its own sake and others placing no special premium upon industriousness. Among individual members of some societies, including our own, achievement is exalted to the point of obsession. For these people, means have become ends, and the reward for their efforts may be principally or solely the feeling of accomplishment or simply knowing that they have not been idle. Our expression "busy work" is illustrative and finds neither counterpart nor comprehension in many other societies.

Industry and achievement continue to be moral values in the United States and, at least in the past, much support for them has been provided by Protestantism. Rather than being the wellspring for the set of values called the Protestant ethic, however, religion may be seen here in its customary role of providing a forceful validation and rationale for sociocultural conditions arising from other sources.

The role of religion is then seen once again as being essentially derivative, although its force as a sanctioning agent may be powerful.

We may note that in the modern United States, the scholarly name for the Protestant ethic has become known as "motivation toward achievement" and most studies of this subject have given little attention to religious ideology. While not explicitly denying the relevance of religion, these studies most frequently center on other factors of seeming significance. The relative strength of motivation toward achievement has been linked with traits such as self-esteem, risk taking, achievement in school, conforming behavior, competition versus cooperation, the value placed upon independence, esthetic and perceptual sensitivity, affiliation with social classes, the nature of familial relations, and ways of training children for roles as adults.

Circumstances in Japan with regard to motivation toward achievement provide an illuminating comparison with Western attitudes bearing on the question of the role of religion in this matter. Japan is unquestionably an example of an achieving nation, and among the people of Japan work and achievement unquestionably have moral value. Diligence, thrift, asceticism, and achievement are Japanese ideals that curiously resemble the Protestant ethic of the Western world. Economic, social, and religious circumstances of Japan's past and present do not, however, closely resemble those of the West. Modern scholarly attempts to understand the origin and maintenance of the Japanese drive toward achievement have seen religion, in the past if not today, as giving some support to achievement as a value, but, like the relationship in general between religion and morality in Japan, the drive to achieve is not seen as intimately linked with religion. The functional counterparts of the independence, individualism, competition, and low degree of parental authority held to be associated with achievement in the United States appear to be reversed in Japan. Japanese society is characterized by strong dependence upon other people, cooperation favored over competition, and parental authority so surrounded and masked by emotional dependence that compliance with parental wishes is more desirable than revolt. In particular, the role of the Japanese mother in rearing her children is seen as important. The strong emotional dependence upon the mother, inculcated by modes of rearing children, is seen to make her an especially potent force in instilling and maintaining a drive toward achievement.

Many linkages may be seen in other societies of the world between religion and economic achievement, and these are variously positive or negative, stimulating or inhibiting economic activities and development. The counterpart of the Protestant ethic fortified by religious sanctions may be found in at least a few primitive societies, as, for example, among the Manus of Melanesia, where ancestral spirits sanction economic productivity. Religious customs of many societies may be seen to have effects upon their economy. Food taboos, such as prohibitions against eating meat, prevent efficient use of available resources, and the long religious holidays characteristic of many societies similarly inhibit economic production. Great religious festivals that require extraordinary amounts of foods and other goods are stimuli to economic activities. When an overall view is taken of these customs, the conclusion accords with that of the general relationship between morality and religion. Productive work and economic achievement may or may not be moral issues and may or may not be matters of religion.

5

Transcendence

Transcendence of ordinary psychic states is a universal trait of religion that takes many forms. Transcendental states have often been actively sought as acts of piety. They have also been given religious interpretations of other kinds and have been put to religious use. Like morality in its relation to religion, transcendence is not inherently religious. In man's history, religion has pervaded every aspect of human life and, in doing so, has often claimed or appeared to be the fountainhead of both ideals and acts. Remarkable psychic states that transcend the ordinary are part of the normal behavior of man; that is, they are capabilities and proclivities of the species *Homo sapiens* that are innate and genetically transmitted.

We have given to these states many names that include fantasy, escape, drunkenness, drug trips, play, and, in a religious context, the religious thrill, ecstasy, Nirvana, trance, mysticism, vision, and revelation. Some of the kinds of behavior implied by these names we brand as acceptable, proper, or desirable, and other kinds we call foibles, delusions, and moral failings, sometimes altering our judgments from age to age.

MODES OF RELIGIOUS TRANSCENDENCE

From childhood to death, human beings regularly and actively seek to break the pattern of ordinary states of psychic being and pass through what Aldous Huxley has called "the doors of perception" leading to extraordinary psychic states. Each society defines the modes of transcendence that are acceptable and unacceptable, and religion has often provided a mantle of legitimacy for some or many of these states, allowing, encouraging, or requiring them and, at the same time, exercising control over them. The nature of transcendental behavior is concealed from many Westerners by attitudes of disapproval of certain forms of transcendence that are incorporated in the teachings of the very religion that allows and exalts transcendence interpreted as acts of piety.

Religious transcendence is known to all societies and varies from mild feelings of mystic well-being and rapport with the supernatural to violent seizures and trance. Great Asian religions have had transcendence as their central themes, and in the West the religious thrill has often been described as the core of religion. Extreme transcendence or ecstasy—in ordinary phraseology, the psychic state when one is "beside oneself"—is often an outstanding feature of the religions of both primitive and civilized societies. In many societies, the ability to enter trance has been a requirement for religious specialization. The sign of the calling is psychically remarkable behavior, most commonly long periods of listlessness, illness, and mental instability, culminating in seizures and trance.

Many accounts of the native religions of Siberia, North America, Africa, and other parts of the world describe behavior of this kind among those who become the religious leaders, and similar behavior is well recorded in the religious histories of the great nations of Europe and Asia. Biographies and autobiographies of the majority of the founders of the many "new" religious sects of Japan, founded in the nineteenth and twentieth centuries, describe events of this classic pattern in the early history of the lives of these men and women. Their behavior is distinctive only in being moderate rather than extreme, a circumstance wholly in keeping with the moderation of behavior of all kinds which characterizes the Japanese population. These traits of religious specialists are so common that anthropologists many years ago adopted the name *shaman*, derived from the native term in one of the Siberian languages, to label the inspired religious specialist who employs ecstatic states and acquires supernatural power by vision or revelation.

Most frequently, the signs of the call to religious specialization are regarded as a supernatural mandate. The call must be heeded or else misfortune of one kind or another will follow. Once the signs of the calling clearly appear, the course of action of the inspired future specialist in religion is everywhere the same. He must learn how to control ecstasy, entering trance at will whenever the demands of his office require it and leaving trance when his religious tasks of communicating with the supernatural are finished. Some practitioners develop techniques of control by themselves but the most common procedure is to seek the training of an established specialist who has mastered all of the necessary skills. As a gifted religious specialist, the trained shaman then serves his fellow men, advising them with supernatural assistance and thereby providing them with psychological assurance. Many religions, great and obscure, may be traced historically to the ecstatic revelations of such inspired prophets.

Ecstasy is not the exclusive prerogative of religious specialists, of course, although these men and women may make the greatest use of it and claim the ability to attain it as an exclusive, divine gift. The cultural patterning of ecstatic states is clearly evident in the identity of the participants as well as in the behavior of ecstasy. In some societies only men enter trance and are religious specialists; in other societies only women do so; and in some societies only the children of established shamans receive the call to religious specialization.

Ecstasy through religion may be open to all and is sometimes expected or required of all at certain times in life or on certain ritual occasions. Revelations or divine visions have been extremely common religious phenomena and imply ecstasy. In every society, visions and revelations are culturally conventionalized. As we have seen, the individual Indian of the Great Plains received supernatural power, and often also a guardian spirit, from a vision or hallucination induced by extreme self-torture. Most frequently the Indian seeker for power performed his acts in solitude. In other societies, transcendence may be sought jointly, as a customary part of established ritual or for special goals. In Bali, large numbers of adult males and females enter trance together while performing elaborate ceremonial dances in which motor behavior, the use of the feet, arms, trunk, and head, follows intricate, learned patterns of dance that dramatically reenact myth-ological dramas and end in violent seizures in which behavior is also patterned. While in ecstasy, thousands of Americans who were members of the church groups of the Kentucky Revival of the nineteenth century ran about on all fours, making barking sounds, and "treeing the Devil." In Christian tradition as well as in the religious practices of many other societies, primitive and civilized, ecstatics have often "talked in tongues," uttering sounds interpreted variously as the languages of the gods or spirits or other supernaturalistic languages.

In various Asian societies, the nature of such behavior as psychological transport or transcendence is clearly manifest to the ecstatics and is sometimes explicitly taught as a cherished benefit or goal of religion. The "dance of ecstasy" (*muga no mai*) of a modern, if unusual, sect of Japan reflects ancient religious ideas of both India and China, and its etymology states an ancient Asian goal of religion. In direct translation the title of the dance, in part derived from Chinese, is "dance of no self" or "dance of selflessness." Again in keeping with Japanese modes, the dance of selflessness is a mild form of ecstasy and it does not end in seizures and catalepsy. In the modern United States, religious ecstasy in violent form, although less common than in the past, remains a central feature of the practices of both ministers and lay members of some Christian sects.

Techniques for achieving ecstasy are also numerous and similarly follow distinc-tive patterns in each society. Suggestion and autosuggestion are doubtless always involved. For shamans, trance is usually so induced. Many mechanical means are also used that alter physiological processes and affect auditory and visual perception. Throughout the world, the most common mechanical procedure is deprivation of bodily necessities, especially food. Fasts and religious revelations have a long history of intimate connection. Control of respiration and bodily torture by incision, flagellation, and violent physical exertion are other techniques. The American Indian of the Great Plains seeking a vision might insert skewers in his flesh, tying to them by thongs the skulls of buffalos, which he then dragged behind him. In the visionary rite called the Sun Dance, he tethered himself by skewers and thongs to a pole around which he danced without pause while staring at the sun.

Many substances were taken internally to induce visions, of which the most important were a large number of hallucinatory plant drugs including marihuana, hallucinogenic mushrooms, and the cactus *peyote*. Many such plant substances were used ritually in aboriginal times by Indians of both North and, especially, South America and some continue to be used today.

What appears most striking in the relationship between transcendental states and religion is that religion has provided a vehicle for transcendence and has at the same time controlled it in ways that foster the well-being of the individual without leading to social disruption. Religion has defined the states in ways that are socially acceptable or desirable. Until modern times, for example, seizures and trance were not the neurotic or psychotic acts of the emotionally unstable. They were instead evidence of possession by spiritual beings, a gift of grace that was put to social use. When possession was seen as invasion by evil spiritual beings, the remarkable behavior placed no burden of blame for psychic malfunction on the afflicted. In most instances, transcendence is desired and actively sought. In ways about which we yet know little, it appears to be necessary or somehow rewarding to those who seek and achieve it. Religion has often clearly told the members of society, when, where, how, and how often to reach these states.

Transcendence is not limited to the religious thrill but, as our partial inventory of names given to transcendence notes, includes the wide range of activities that we ordinarily call play. Human play may be seen, in fact, to include with many other activities the states of being and acts called religious ecstasy, and the discussion of human play which follows will serve to expand upon the subject of religious ecstasy. Many activities of play have similarly been religiously sponsored and controlled. This does not mean to imply that religion has always fostered or regarded play in ways that are individually and socially supportive. The religious creed of the West that we have discussed as the Protestant ethic has been remarkable in its opposition to play as well as to transcendence in any other of its forms except those regarded as religion.

HUMAN PLAY AND RELIGION[1]

As we have earlier noted, the set of values called the Protestant ethic is far from extinct in the United States today. Devotion to work was traditionally a virtue, and play was the enemy of work, reluctantly and charily permitted only to children. The old admonition that play is the devil's handiwork continues to have life in secular attitudes. Although play has now become almost respectable, it is still something in which we "indulge," a form of moral laxness. We have also already noted that in many societies work is seldom valued for its own sake. The evidence seems to state that most people in most times have not worked hard and that a sustained cycle of hard work is a phenomenon of modern times limited principally to the industrialized, "modern" nations of the world. For even the most primitive peoples who live by hunting and gathering wild foods, life does not seem to have consisted of unremitting hard work to scratch out a bare livelihood. The modern !Kung tribe of Bushmen of the Kalahari Desert in Africa, for example, have been shown to work only twelve to nineteen hours weekly to provide for themselves. A recent anthropological work puts the beginning of lengthy and regular work as following man's invention of plant and animal husbandry, perhaps ten thousand years ago, when planned programs of regular labor became necessary for economic success and when small children could be put regularly to economically useful tasks such as tending livestock.

Attitudes toward play of many societies also differ from those prevailing in the United States today and, especially, from our attitudes of the recent past. In most societies, play has not been a sin or even a foible. It has instead been an outstanding and socially approved feature of life that has often held a position of honor as a central theme of religious observances. The idea that play is frivolity and not the proper, serious business of life has a history of some centuries in Europe and the United States, and it has doubtless played a part in spurring the economic and scientific development of our nation. The neglect of human play as an

[1] Thanks are due to *Natural History* for permission to republish in the following pages excerpts from an article by the author, "Man at Play," which appears in the December 1971 issue of *Natural History*.

anthropological subject of study also doubtless reflects this idea. As Margaret Mead has observed, for most social scientists financial support for the study of play among adults has generally been available only when play is called recreation, a label that identifies its role in recreating human beings for the serious and proper business of life. But human play need not be regarded simply as restful diversion from more important activities or as the behavior of children. Play is both a biological and sociocultural phenomenon that we are now beginning to see as having significance of many kinds, some of which concern modern social problems.

We easily recognize play as characteristic of nonhuman species as well as of *Homo sapiens*. When one dog chases another and the roles are suddenly reversed so that the pursuer becomes the pursued, we instantly see the behavior as play. A distinctive combination of traits distinguishes play from other acts. For all forms of life, play may be defined as voluntary, pleasurable behavior that is separated in time from other activities and has a quality of make-believe. Play is thus a form of transcendence, behavior that closely resembles religious transcendence, which may itself be called a form of play. Human play differs uniquely from that of other species, however, because it is molded by culture, consciously and unconsciously. That is, human play, like religious trancendence, is conditioned by learned attitudes and values which have no counterpart among nonhuman species.

Following our definition, forms of human play include sports and games of all kinds, dancing, singing, wit and humor, dramas, comedies, theatrical performances and other forms of mimicry, art, music, and other branches of esthetics, induced states of psychological transcendence such as those resulting from drinking alcohol and using drugs that alter the sensibilities, and religious ecstasy, however induced.

From the research of biologists and primatologists, it is clear that play is innate behavior in the entire class of mammals, so well established and recognizable that play sometimes occurs between individuals of different species. Among the many forms of mammalian life, however, man is the supreme player. Forms of human play tend to change as human beings age, but man appears to play most intensely and in the greatest variety of ways, and to be the only species in the entire mammalian class which plays conspicuously from birth to death. Some human societies have discouraged many or most forms of play and have prohibited certain forms, such as dancing, but the impulse to play is irrepressible, appearing unmistakably in every normal, new-born child. Children love to be swung by their hands in circles until they are dizzy and to visit amusement parks in order to ride roller coasters and other similar devices that derange the sensibilities or provide thrilling experiences.

The biological and evolutionary adaptive significance of mammalian play is unknown, but it appears to have vital neurophysiological effects. Itself a change in pace, it occurs, transitorily, when changes in pace come about. Among human beings, play may be seen as linked with discontinuities, such as changes in kinds of work, the completion of any time-consuming project that concentrates on one kind of activity, and changes in social states with attendant changes in behavior. The great annual festivals of human societies commonly occur at junctures in the annual cycles of economic activity, such as breaking ground, planting, and harvest, and these, in turn, are connected with changes in the seasons. The traditional Christian festivals may be traced to such times in the agricultural calendar of the eastern Mediterranean lands where Christianity emerged. Play behavior included in rites of birth, coming of age, marriage, and funerals takes place at a time when human roles change: the youth becomes an adult; the single girl becomes a wife; the childless woman becomes a mother; and the bereaved wife becomes a widow while her deceased spouse becomes a disembodied spirit. These changes in status entail changes in behavior on the part of both the subjects of ritual and those with whom they have social contacts.

Why northern European societies attempted to suppress human play cannot be explained through religion. Religion was the rationale for suppression but the circumstances fostering this rationale are unclear. We may note that suppression of innate behavior is not limited to play. In all human societies, and perhaps especially in societies holding the Christian view that man is a special creation, any behavior that calls attention to the nature of man as an animal is strongly conditioned, controlled, or even suppressed. All necessary bodily functions such as eating, drinking, excreting, breathing and sleeping are bound by firm conventions and should ordinarily be performed as unobtrusively as possible. It was scarcely possible to imagine that beneath the demeanor and substantial garb of the Victorian lady lay a busy alimentary canal. Ponder for a moment the probable effect on the careers of politicians, ministers, or university professors of flatulence in public or the frank scratching in the presence of spectators of certain parts of the body. Human copulation was for many reasons unseemly behavior, so animal-like that the anatomical reminders of sexuality were concealed by garments that sometimes remarkably altered contours of the body—and led to amazing symbols of eroticism.

These and other suppressions of man–animal behavior have been important and, in the sense that we and our culture would otherwise be very different, were probably required in the biological evolution of man and the development of society and culture. As anthropologists have often said, man domesticated himself. The trend toward suppressing the beast within reached its greatest height in Europe and the United States, where it includes attempts to suppress play as a matter of morality. Only very recently have we been able to think that perhaps we went too far, creating for ourselves a complex of social problems. The past few decades might realistically be called the age of man's rediscovery of his animal nature.

Elsewhere in the world among people of simpler ways of life, and among ourselves in the not-very-distant past, play has been wholly acceptable behavior and —it is now possible to say—potential problems of unregulated play did not exist in the societies because play was institutionalized. All types of play existed and were permitted under conditions of regulation that kept them in order and, in ways that I shall try to make clear, contributed to social harmony and personal well-being. The most important means of regulation of the past was to make forms of play into religious activities that were permitted or even required on certain fixed occasions. Anthropological knowledge of the forms of play of the various societies of the world is imperfect, but it is safe to say that all forms I have listed exist in every historically known society.

One of the most common examples of play in religious dress is the rite of reversal, a festival of upside-downing during which the social hierarchy is inverted, customary rules of moral behavior are suspended, and other ordinary behavior, such as the direction of walking and dancing, is done "backward." Commoners may insult kings; women may deride men; and resentments of all kinds may be expressed with impunity. Obscenity, lewdness, sexual license, theft, and assault or mock assault may all be permissible. Mimicry, drama, wit and humor, song, dance, pageantry, and alcoholic drunkenness and other forms of induced euphoric transcendence may all be incorporated in the rites. But let us note that the festivals are not truly chaotic. Order prevails in seeming disorder. Reversals begin and end at fixed times; all participants know the rules, and all are well aware of the qualities of make-believe and transitoriness of the festival behavior.

Rites of reversal—a subject to be discussed in greater detail in the following chapter—faded away as Western civilization spread from Europe, but they were once widespread and they continue to exist in many societies. Many of these rites are fundamentally complexes of forms of play. Although once common in northern Europe, the birthplace of the Protestant ethic, the rites linger there today as religious events only as variably strong echoes among the Roman Catholic segment. They are still practiced in South America and elsewhere where Roman Catholicism is strong. Their absence in the United States except in the faint afterglow of the Mardi Gras of New Orleans is not surprising.

It is not difficult to see positive implicit functions in the religious sanction of these forms of play; that is, the rites promote well-being and social order in various ways of which the participants are unaware. The rites may be easily seen as safety valves for both individuals and social groups. Many Americans might see such value in an African rite which allowed men to berate their mothers-in-law. The return to ordinary rules of behavior after a departure from them may also reasonably be seen as affirmations or reaffirmations of the propriety of the everyday rules. The rites also provide, with social approval and encouragement, opportunities for esthetic expression as well as for other forms of play. Permissiveness accompanied by control prevents play from getting out of hand. I am aware of no report on primitive societies under native conditions of life that even suggest play is a social problem.

One of our difficulties has been that our attitudes toward play have not dimmed our impulses to play. Even when it was held in the greatest disfavor, we continued to play—unobtrusively, by recourse to the least disfavored forms of play and, often enough, surreptitiously, illegally, and with feelings of guilt. Of course, not all people were taken in by the prevailing conventions and continued to play, and some of us have been able to regard our work as play.

An acute social problem facing us today concerns a form of play that we have seldom recognized as play, and which other societies have been able to handle by regarding as normal if remarkable behavior and as a religious act. As we have noted, transcendental states are not a corrupt innovation of modern youth but are ancient among human beings everywhere and have often included transcendence through the use of drugs. We have also noted that where transcendence by the use of drugs is socially acceptable religious customs often serve as a means of control. American Indian members of the congregations of the legally chartered Native American Church have for decades sought transcendence as a religious act during weekly ceremonies. This is done by eating peyote, a small, spineless cactus that contains mescaline. This custom appears to have brought neither addictive craving nor social disturbance. In modern India, the drinking of liquid concoctions of marihuana is similarly religious, a part of the traditional festival of Holī, and is thus similarly permitted and controlled by convention.

Circumstances surrounding the use of psychedelic drugs in the modern United States differ outstandingly in a number of ways. As with many other forms of play in the United States, the use of drugs is a moral offense, intimately tied with the religious tradition, and this attitude is generally held by even the nonreligious part of the population. Disapproved by most people and prohibited by law, the use of drugs in the United States lacks peaceful modes of control and is left for regulation to the force of law.

Much of the foregoing has been to say that in play as well as in other things the whole world is not like Dubuque, Iowa, or New York City and that the transition to modern civilization has brought losses as well as gains. But the intent is to say still more. We have seen something of the ways that societies have regarded and handled play, some providing for it a place of honor and putting it to social use, if unwittingly. Other societies, notably our own in recent centuries, have held play in dishonor, a course of action that has borne positive results in monumental economic achievements but, at the same time, has presented us with a train of social problems.

The complex record of Christianity is not, however, one of stern prohibition of all forms of play except religious ecstasy. Like religions elsewhere in the world, it has been a major vehicle for all of the forms of esthetics, sometimes prohibiting certain forms, such as representations in painting or statuary depicting biblical figures, but generally providing rich encouragement for others. As elsewhere, these have been regarded as devotional or otherwise religiously commendable activities.

6

Group Rites

No comprehensive and convenient classification of rites of supernaturalism is in general use. The most general terms are rite, ritual, and ceremony, which mean any established procedures or conventionalized acts of supernaturalism. Specific names, such as totemic rites, first fruit ceremonies, and rites of circumcision are plentiful for types of rites which refer to the actual purpose of the procedure or to the occasions requiring it. Rites so classified have not been systematically placed in any general or comprehensive taxonomy and various features often overlap. For example, funerals are commonly classified as one of the rites of passage, a classification which includes a number of subtypes, all of which have the common feature of celebrating social transitions of one kind or another of individual members of society. But funerals, or other rites of passage, may include or consist of procedures known in other contexts by other names, such as rites of ancestor worship, rites of the dead, commemorative rites, rites of reversal, sacrificial rites, and a large number of magical rites.

Compiling a list of the many names given to rites would be a time-consuming task and, for the purposes of this book, would have little value. Preceding chapters have described the whole assemblage of rites of supernaturalism in two distinguishable general categories, rites of magic or mechanical formulas thought to control the supernatural and acts toward personified supernatural beings. We have already noted that these distinguishable types of acts are frequently incorporated in a single ceremony. Christian services of worship, for example, may include the magical sacrament of Communion. So also with other distinguishable types of rites. Many may be incorporated in a single ceremony. We have also noted that anthropological interpretations of magic and of rites toward a personified universe have been alike in their assumptions about the significance of the rites and in their procedures of interpretation. Primary emphasis has been given to the social significance of the acts and this has been judged by examining the acts in their sociocultural context.

By custom or requirement, many rites are the joint activities of social groups, such as the family and, in primitive societies, lineages, clans, and other large kin groupings, the community, and the entire society. A lesser number of rites, including many but not all acts of magic, are performed by individuals acting in their own personal interests, although the significance of these rites always extends in some measure beyond the individual to the social group. The pages which follow will accordingly be concerned principally with rites that are performed by groups, whether large or small. No attempt will be made to discuss all or even many of the types of rites to which names have been given. Instead, classes of rites are chosen as examples, both of rites and of anthropological handling of them. The four categories of rites selected for discussion, cyclic rites, rites of passage, rites of healing, and rites of reversal are not always mutually exclusive; that is, like other classes of rites they may include some elements in common. As a group, they cover a large part of the total roster of ritual acts, however named, that are observed throughout the world. Three of the four categories are universal. The fourth, the rite of reversal, is common but not universal and has been selected as exemplary of a current line of anthropological interpretation.

A summary of the foregoing prefatory remarks is useful: It is impossible and scarcely useful to discuss in a few pages all named types of rites. All hold much in common in their contents and all are treated anthropologically in essentially the same way. The preceding chapters have already discussed rites of magic, including witchcraft, and various other classes of rites. This chapter amplifies earlier discussions and selects as its subjects types of rites that appear to be the most suitable because they are both common and have been the subjects of anthropological interpretation.

CYCLIC RITES AND RITES OF PASSAGE

Cyclic rites and rites of passage are fundamentally similar and, in the ideas and acts they include, sometimes identical, but they are distinctive in the events which they celebrate, the times at which they are conducted, and, to a degree, in their social significance.

Cyclic rites are fixed ceremonies observed in all societies that celebrate important times or events. Many of the greatest religious ceremonies relate to the means of gaining a livelihood and, in turn, to the seasons of the year. For many decades, anthropologists describing the religions of primitive societies have used the classification "ceremonial calendar" to describe these fixed ceremonies, which are intimately tied to the economic cycle. These rites mark the beginning or end of particular kinds of human activities or cycles of life. Common examples are rites that celebrate annual migrations of fish and game, the clearing of agricultural land, planting, harvest, and the beginning of a new year. In some societies, the end of the old year is also celebrated. In literate societies with organized priesthoods where religious activities are conducted principally by religious specialists, cyclic ceremonies often observe great events in the religious history such as the birth and death of prophets.

The range of rites or kinds of ritual acts comprehended by the label "cyclic rites" is enormous, including fertility rites, first fruits ceremonies, ceremonies to bring rain, annual rites of world renewal that assure successful living in the coming year, hunting and fishing rites, and rites of thanksgiving. Most of these ceremonies are familiar in the modern Western world, and, if their prevalence in primitive societies is evidence of antiquity, they must be very ancient. Varying from society to society, the cyclic rites we have named were all observed, for example, by North American Indians in aboriginal times and some continue to be observed by them today. At the beginning of the annual runs of salmon, Indians of the northwest coast who lived by hunting, fishing, and gathering wild vegetable foods held elaborate rites honoring the spirits of the salmon. Horticultural Pueblo Indians of the arid southwest continue today to conduct annual ceremonies to bring rain. The "green corn ceremony" of horticultural Indians east of the Mississippi River was a first fruits ceremony, which required as one of its elements the purification of people, through a ritual which included use of a plant emetic, before they could eat the first new corn. Cyclic rites are so well represented in the traditional ceremonies of the United States and Europe that added examples seem unnecessary.

Rites of passage are also well established in the Western religious tradition, but the full range of these rites does not exist in the United States today. As earlier passages have stated, rites of passage celebrate important events in the lives of individuals, marking the passage to new social statuses of the individuals upon whom they center. Many are connected with the biological crises of life, birth, maturation, reproduction, and death. The normal cycle of life in a society, however, may involve noteworthy events in addition to birth, coming of age, attaining parenthood, and dying. One may go through many social statuses during both childhood and adult life. For example, primitive societies are sometimes clearly divided by age grades that are socially important. Accession to positions of eminence and authority are also social transitions. Many rites of passage are ceremonies of initiation or inauguration into such special social groups.

In his classic book *The Rites of Passage*, first published in French in 1912, Arnold van Gennep noted three stages in these rites, *separation, transition,* and *reincorporation.* Accounts of hundreds of rites observed today or in the recent past show these steps or stages clearly. The people upon whom the rites focus are first symbolically, and often physically, separated from the rest of society. They must then for a period of time act in extraordinary ways, and they are finally, symbolically, and actually reincorporated in society in their new statuses, very often equipped with visible symbols of the new status in the form of tattoos, scars, rings, clothing, ornaments, distinctive styles of hairdress, and badges of office.

Among the symbols indicating attainment of adulthood are alterations of the genital organs that cannot be called surgery because their goals are social rather than therapeutic. Circumcision of males is the most common, but other genital operations including subincision of the urethra are also performed. In some societies of Africa and Western Asia, clitoridectomies and other genital operations were performed and continue to be performed today upon females. The general significance of these operations as indicators of social status seems quite clear from a survey of practices found throughout the world of modifying parts of the body. Lips, ears, and noses are pierced and incised to allow the insertion of ornaments, some of which are huge and remarkably alter the physical appearance of the organs. Canine teeth are removed and incisors are ground to points, and necks are elongated by brass rings encasing them. The skin is decorated by tattoos and, where skins are dark, by incisions into which foreign matter may be inserted to create designs in low relief. Even the form of the head is altered in a number of societies by pressing and binding during childhood. Members of the upper class of some Indian societies of British Columbia molded their skull vaults to a form resembling the end of a chicken's egg. Until recent times the feet of Chinese women were bound, ideally to a length not to exceed three inches. This practice was a symbol of social status; women with bound feet were members of an elite class who did not do productive economic work. No part of the human body that is not vital for survival in the natural form has escaped permanent or temporary alteration by some society, and the altered forms are usually seen as giving beauty as well as serving as symbols of status.

A modern trend of interpretation seemingly derived from Freudian psychology sees practices of circumcision as linked with sexual rivalry between father and son over the mother (Whiting, *et al.* 1958).[1] Long intimate association of the male child with the mother accompanied by the prohibition of sexual intercourse between the parents for two or more years after childbirth are seen as correlated with harsh ordeals and genital operations when sons come of age. These ritualized acts are held to break the bond between mother and son, and, without social disruption, to avoid the potential conflict between father and son. This interpretation does not consider genital operations performed on females and seems doubtful for other reasons that are more directly relevant. Among these is the age at which genital operations are performed, which among societies observing this custom ranges from early infancy to about twenty years of age. In native Samoa, for example, circumcision was performed at any age from three to twenty.

Other symbolic acts that are common in rites of passage are ceremonial death followed by rebirth and maturation in the new status. This theme is also common in annual cyclic rites that renew the world. In some societies of Africa, paramount chiefs and kings were symbolically killed annually, sometimes by actual blows on the head, and then symbolically reborn. This custom may be seen as linked with African and Mediterranean customs of actually killing kings when they appeared to be declining physically.

Ordeals are common as a part of coming-of-age ceremonies and they often include extremely unusual behavior. Our example (p. 4) of catching water bugs in the mouth is representative. The ordeal is dramatic and very memorable, but it is possible to undergo the rite successfully. Ordeals are sometimes fearfully thrilling with little danger, but occasionally they do appear to be genuinely dangerous. An ancient Japanese rite for males at age sixteen that is still observed by a few rural people required that the initiate be tied with ropes and lowered head first over the edge of a high cliff. The ordeal was thrilling but so many precautions against injury were taken that no danger was involved. On Pentecost Island in Melanesia the ordeal for a young man is a leap from a high tower with a rope secured about the legs to break the fall just before reaching the ground. Even here permanent injuries seem to be few. In general, ordeals at initiation may be described as memorable symbols of success attained by all. It seems unlikely that in all of history many people have failed to pass their puberty tests.

The general significance of cyclic rites and rites of passage to the individual and to society differs principally in degree. Cyclic rites may be said to have equal significance for all members of the social group concerned. Since rites of passage center on an individual or a small number of persons—for example, coming-of-age rites may be held jointly for all young men and women reaching the appropriate age in a given year—they may be said to have greater significance for the individual

---

[1] For a somewhat similar and more recent interpretation that stresses the social significance of symbolism in rites at coming of age, see Young (1965) listed in Recommended Readings.

than for the group. Both kinds of rites are seen to be societally integrative through the joint beliefs and actions they entail. These may prominently include explicit statement and dramatization, under a mantle of religious symbolism, of moral values thought necessary for the welfare of the individual in his new status and for the entire group in the activities normally pursued by them throughout the year. The social order—relations between people of hierarchy, equality, or of other special nature—is seen to be reenacted by the roles assigned to persons in the rites and is thus seen to be reinforced by the special sanction of religion.

Interpretation of the couvade, described in our Introduction, as an example of unusual behavior, is illustrative. The "classic couvade," in which the father of a newborn child rather than the mother is the center of ritual attention, is widely but unevenly distributed throughout the world. Among Indian tribes of the Amazonian jungle it was rationalized by beliefs of affinity between the soul of the child and his father. Any normal motor activity by the father, such as hunting, fishing, or crossing streams, endangered the soul and the life of the infant for some days after birth. The implicit function having social significance in this custom is its symbolic representation and endorsement of the bonds that should ideally exist between father and child and between father and mother. The simulation of childbirth by the father is an example of imitative magic. By simulating successful childbirth, the father symbolically assures success of the actual birth and, at the same time, provides psychological assurance for all concerned.

By means of similar acts of magic and by symbolism of many kinds, both cyclical rites and rites of passage provide assurance of success in general societal activities such as agriculture and fishing or in matters of importance to individuals. The symbols employed in rites of passage assure success in the new social statuses, which are given both societal and supernatural approval by the rites, and thus they ease the transition to the new social positions.

Rites of passage often explicitly give instruction in the new roles in ways that may be seen as socially supportive. In rites of initiation, such as entering adulthood or joining a social club or religious group, they often give instruction in matters that are earlier unknown to the initiates, but greater social importance is attributed to instruction of another sort. The rites tell the initiates and other members of society of the changes in their relationships and clearly instruct all concerned how to conduct themselves. In rites of mourning, for example, the bereaved receive psychologically supporting attention and sympathy and also instructions that are essentially commands. Their grief is pointed up by many acts; they are instructed to mourn dramatically, to undergo a period of adjustment, and, at the end of the ritual sequence, they are officially returned to normal society with the unspoken command to put grief behind and act in normal fashion once again. Activities at this time are often joyous behavior, complete with feasts and dancing.

As the preceding references to the dramatization of grief suggest, the idea of the safety valve is also used in interpreting some of the acts of cyclic rites and rites of passage. "Capture" of the bride is a standardized feature of many societies of Africa and is observed in many other parts of the world. The fading American custom of the shivaree (charivari) appears to be an altered survivor of practices of this kind. The sham battles involved in the "capture" of a bride dramatically symbolize and allow controlled expression of the conflict and hostility that actually exist between the two battling ingroups, the relatives of the bride and of the groom. It is noteworthy that in some societies of Africa such controlled sham fighting between relatives of brides and grooms may be the custom at group rites other than weddings for some years after the marriage has taken place. As with other forms of play, religion may be seen here as approving and at the same time controlling.

Although cyclic rites and rites of passage everywhere are regarded as having the same general significances, many questions arise about differences in the rites from society to society. Rites at marriage or at coming of age might, for example, be simple or extremely elaborate among societies of seemingly equal levels of cultural development with economic bases that seem essentially identical. Attempts to explain the presence or absence, different degrees of elaboration, and distinctive features of rites have followed the prevailing anthropological trend; that is, they have relied principally upon examination of the social order, often as it relates to economic matters. Conclusions of most of these interpretations may be summarized briefly in the truism that the degree of ritual attention depends upon the social and related psychological importance of the events in question. The problem has been to understand what it is that makes the events socially and psychologically important or unimportant, to comprehend such things as the kinds of social circumstances that make lasting marriages vitally important or relatively unimportant and the social conditions that make the transition to adulthood a simple procedure or one fraught with social and psychological conflicts and stresses.

Some reasonable interpretations accounting for differences in rites have been offered. The simple ceremonies of marriage found in matrilineal societies, for example, reflect the relative lack of importance of marriage unions in these societies, in which divorce is simple and comparatively common. In these societies, descent is traced through female lines only and membership in important social groups such as lineages and clans is based upon kinship so reckoned. The cooperating kin groups are then composed of male and female adults and children united by matrilineal descent. Marriage is exogamous; that is, spouses must be from a matrilineal kin group other than one's own. Where, as in many matrilineal societies, gaining a livelihood, rearing children, and other normal activities of life are the functions of the matrilineal kin group, the husband and father is an outsider. His primary ties are with his sisters, their children, his brothers, and his other matrilineal kin. Matrilineal societies vary considerably in the roles given to the husband–father with respect to his wife and children. At the extreme of emphasis on matrilineal ties he is only the sexual consort of his wife and the procreator of his children, and spends most of his time with his own matrilineal kin. In societies such as this, in which the mother's brother or brothers are the economic providers and adult male socializers for children, the end of a marriage causes little social disruption. The economic welfare, social affiliation, and primary human relationships of children are unchanged by divorce and the divorced mother suffers less change in these important matters than in societies otherwise socially ordered.

Rites of marriage are generally more elaborate in societies in which descent is traced through male lines, and people take their affiliation with kin groups accordingly. Strong sanctions, often including supernatural sanctions, foster lasting unions of marriage, which are vital to the continuation of society. The mother, who is an outsider from another patrilineal kin group of the society, is necessary for the rearing of children. Women of the husband's patrilineal kin group cannot ordinarily fill roles with respect to the wife's children that are the female counterparts of the male roles of the mother's brother. Sanctions for the unions are often multiple in these societies. Divorce initiated by women is difficult or impossible; it may be disgraceful or otherwise troublesome for a wife to return to life with her natal kin group; and elaborate procedures of contracting a marriage may include the transfer of valuable goods to the family of the bride, goods that must be returned if the marriage falls asunder. Grand festivities of marriage that include supernatural sanctions of the union are also common.

In societies such as our own, where descent is traced through both male and female lines and the small family of husband, wife, and children is the only kin unit of importance, lasting marriages are also vital. The importance of the family with respect to the economic, social, and psychological well-being of children is obvious, but many economic and other factors operate to make unions of marriage brittle. We may note, however, that the sanctions for lasting unions in the United States are particularly abundant. In addition to religious and secular rites of marriage, informal sanctions against divorce that relate to social prestige are plentiful if variable, and a vast, intricate network of legal sanctions concerns divorce and familial property. The negative sanctions on divorce that are traditional, and still alive, in our society seem to be curiously and ethnocentrically reflected in scholarly accounts of rites of passage. Most frequently, divorce is not included among these rites, although observances, generally simple and quite secular, that celebrate divorce are common enough.

A question that springs to mind in connection with the uneven distribution throughout the world of rites of passage is the absence or near-absence of rites at coming of age in our own society. No established rites of this kind are generally observed by the entire population, although some Jewish people still observe the ceremony of Bar Mitzvah and the ceremonies of confirmation are conducted for adolescents by some Christian churches. Western tradition once had well-developed rites of this kind, but these and many other rites seem to have been suppressed as the undesirable "holy play of heathens." Other circumstances also discourage the observance of these rites today. Coming of age is associated with puberty—the observances are often called puberty rites—and even the word "puberty" was scarcely acceptable for many years because it referred to the forbidden topic of sex. Still other circumstances of modern life make general rites of coming of age inappropriate in the United States. In our complex society with its elaborate specialization of labor and associated differences in social statuses and levels of formal education, the age at which one becomes socially mature is mysterious. Legal ages at which one may marry with or without parental consent, own property, vote, purchase tobacco and alcoholic drinks, drive an automobile, and at which one is inducted into military service vary considerably. If social maturity is reckoned as the time at which one becomes a self-supporting, contributing member of society, much of our population is immature until the age of about twenty-two, when college training is over, and those who go on for advanced scientific or scholarly training are immature for several additional years. These circumstances present multiple problems manifested in the social and psychological turmoil so common among adolescents and young adults in the United States. Where, as in many simpler societies of the world, the transition from the roles of childhood to those of adulthood is clearly defined and easily within the competence of everyone, youthful turmoil and juvenile delinquency are unknown. Rites of transition to adulthood may readily be seen as socially valuable, but they are appropriate only in marking the actual assumption of fully adult roles, an event which the circumstances of our life today often makes difficult and which, for many people, cannot occur until years after they have reached sexual and physical maturity.

RITES OF HEALING

Judging from the circumstances in historically known primitive societies, it seems safe to assume that during nearly all of man's history the realms of medicine and supernaturalism have been either closely associated or identical. In our own history, the bacterial theory of disease is recent, and until recent times ailments of diverse pathogenesis were linked in one way or another with supernaturalism. Recent and modern times have seen a curious compatibility of supernaturalistic and scientific ideas of the causes of diseases and other ailments. In some primitive societies that have accepted the scientific interpretation of germs as the cause of disease, ideas of supernatural causation are still current and are compatible with conditions of modern life for much the same reason as divination continues to be acceptable. A modern member of tribal society may understand that smallpox and diphtheria are caused by germs. To recover his health, he may then take modern medications and follow other practices of scientific medicine. But only supernaturalism can deal with one aspect of his illness, the reasons why he as an individual suffered the misfortune of contracting the disease. Traditional ideas and acts of supernaturalism can tell him whether the illness is the effect of witchcraft, the violation of a taboo, or some unwitting act which brought disease as a supernatural punishment. Somewhat similar ideas connected with morality are traditional in Western society in the ideas of "sins of the father" and sin of any other kind. Until recent times, for example, some opinion held that the contracting of syphilis was a just and supernaturally ordained punishment for sinful behavior.

Links between scientific and supernaturalistic modes of therapy are curiously close, and much of modern medicine may be described as having its beginnings in practices of supernaturalism. From the modern viewpoint, many primitive medical practices provide the right answers for the wrong reasons, but scientific and certain supernaturalistic ideas of pathogenesis do not differ very drastically and the accompanying techniques of therapy hold much in common.

In all historically known primitive societies, the causes of most diseases and other illnesses are thought to be supernatural. Extremely common minor afflictions, such as accidental fractures of the bones and death from old age, are sometimes regarded as "natural," but even these are often laid to the action of supernatural forces. These supernatural forces are by now quite familiar to us, entities with the qualities of human beings, certain acts, and inanimate substances that are either inherently harmful or somehow bring illness by supernatural means. The most common theory of pathogenesis may be reduced to a single brief statement: entry into the human body by spiritual beings or foreign substances. Perhaps it does not stretch the imagination too far to see this view as the supernaturalistic counterpart of scientific ideas of diseases caused by viruses and germs. Other fairly common supernaturalistic ideas of the causes of disease are moral breaches, the violation of taboos, and witchcraft. Immorality and the breaking of taboos may bring illness as personified punishment levied by supernatural beings or it may come as the inevitable result of violating taboos, without the intervention of supernatural beings. The violation of some taboos brings illness as the result of contact with supernaturally harmful substances. Witchcraft operates to cause illness by any of these means; the witch may cause spirits and substances to enter the victim's body or he may simply project harmful influence.

Supernatural practices of therapy accord with the ideas of pathogenesis. When illness is thought to be caused by the unwanted invasion of the body by a spirit, techniques of therapy consist of acts that will cause the spirit to leave. All of the behavior of human interpersonal relations is used. Invading spirits are sometimes treated in hospitable, winning ways. Pleas to leave the body are made to them; they are cajoled and flattered, and they are enticed to leave by fine offerings. But the possessing spirits are generally evil beings, and coercive acts are more common. The body of the afflicted is made as uncomfortable as possible and other forcible techniques of ejection are used. As in traditional Christian rites of exorcising the devil, expulsion may be in the form of a stern command in the name of a powerful supernatural being. More commonly, mechanical procedures are followed in attempts to make the body inhospitable or otherwise to eject the spirit. Included among the common techniques of expulsion are heating and cooling the body by fire, water, or sweat baths, massage, pummeling, and the forced ingestion of substances that smell or taste bad. Emetics and cathartics of many kinds were also used in an effort to expel invading spirits. In a few societies the spirits could be shocked into leaving. In the Marquesas Islands of Polynesia spirits were shocked into fleeing by the wives of sick men, who jumped naked over the bodies of their husbands. Old customs of venesection or bloodletting of Europe that continued until modern times appear to have been originally derived from ideas of invasion by spirits or substances.

When sickness is caused by the entry of foreign substances, the common technique of cure is to draw the substance out. Techniques of drawing are sometimes symbolic, such as the application of one end of a string to the site of pain while the other end of the string is placed in the curer's mouth. More frequently it is an actual physical act of drawing, accomplished by mechanical devices that make a suction, or, most commonly, by the curer sucking the site of pain with his mouth. The sucking shaman who first supernaturally determines the cause of disease is a common figure in accounts of primitive societies. Evidence of success is often given by the medical practitioner, who, by sleight of hand, displays a stone, stick, thorn, insect, or other small object or form of life that his sucking has drawn out.

Illness as the result of moral failures may often be cured by acts of penitence. Sickness resulting from the violation of taboos may also sometimes be cured by remedial techniques of magic, but in some societies no remedial steps may be taken for either witting or unwitting misdeeds. Since witchcraft cuts across all ideas of the genesis of disease, techniques for recovery from illnesses so caused are correspondingly variable and generally include efforts to neutralize or eradicate the witch.

Surgery is little developed in primitive medicine, and as a developed field it is late in modern medicine. Here and there a few practices of surgery have been reported in primitive societies, and a unique example was discovered by recent archeological investigations in Iraq, which uncovered one skeleton of Neanderthal man with an amputated arm. The lack of development of surgery seems to accord with the ideas of pathogenesis. Much of modern surgery consists of removing diseased organs and thus depends on a theory of pathogenesis that seems to have been rare until recent centuries. One form of surgery has considerable antiquity, however, and a fairly wide distribution. Trephination (also called trepannation), the surgical removal of part of the bone of the skull—cutting a hole in the skull, is known from Neolithic skeletons of the British Isles over 4,000 years old, was also practiced by the ancient Inca and various other societies in the world, and is still performed occasionally by some modern Indians of Chile. This form of surgery may be seen as compatible with the idea of spirit possession.

We are hard put to make an accurate appraisal of the therapeutic value of supernaturalistic techniques of medicine, yet the roots of many modern medical techniques are evident in primitive practices of hydrotherapy, heat therapy, massage, and the use of cathartics and emetics. Supernaturalistic medicine was particularly rich in its pharmacopoeia of plant medications, many of which have been found to be specifically useful for the ailments for which they were prescribed. Native Mexico and Peru alone contributed to European medicine a large number of plant medications, including ipecac and cascara, that were standard remedies until very recent times. Whether or not herbal remedies were actually curative, it seems safe to assume that the psychotherapeutic elements of primitive practices of medicine had consistent value for the ailing.

It is in psychotherapy that the closest links are evident between modern and primitive practices. The Freudian concepts of *id* and *superego* are roughly analogous with ancient ideas of supernatural beings, evil spirits which cause immorality and gods of morality who watch over human behavior. Among the Iroquois Indians of the northeastern United States ideas resembling those of Freud with regard to dreams and repressed desires existed in aboriginal times and were incorporated into religious rites. Annually, the Iroquois conducted a ceremony in which participants were allowed to express repressed desires.

Primitive and modern practices of psychotherapy are closely similar in procedures of handling patients. Both make the afflicted the center of concentrated attention, thereby providing him with psychological support. Both promise or offer palliation or recovery, and both strongly involve healing by faith. Some practices of primitive medicine seem, in fact, psychotherapeutically more valuable than the practices and associated lay attitudes of our own society. Primitive healing tends more than modern medicine to be a joint act involving many people, who provide strong psychic support to the afflicted. Spiritual beings and forces also offer psychological support, and primitive attitudes toward the psychotic characteristically differ from ours in a way that may be seen to promote recovery. The affliction of the psychotic does not put him beyond the pales of society; it is instead a misfortune that may happen to anyone and for which techniques of cure are available. The afflicted thus does not lose the social support of his fellow men, and the native interpretation of the cause of his illness as spirit possession most frequently places no personal blame on the sick person. The Algonquin Indian possessed by the evil spirit called Windigo or Wiitiko was driven by the spirit to desire to commit the horrible offense of cannibalism, but the possessed human being was not regarded as acting willfully and was not held personally accountable for his terrible behavior. Until recent times, Western interpretation of psychosis was also spirit possession, but this possession was by the Devil, often had moral connotations, and resulted in the alienation of the afflicted from the rest of society.

The unintended therapeutic effects of religious customs in many primitive societies with respect to inspired religious specialists seems powerful. Like various of the Christian saints of centuries past, these men and women often appear to have been emotionally unstable. Although we today would regard many of these people as psychiatrically abnormal, in their own societies they are socially normal—and are put to religious use in ways that benefit others and are therapeutically useful to the practitioners themselves.

Primitive and modern psychotherapy are also similar in another respect—for neither set of procedures is it possible to make with assurance an appraisal of cures.

RITES OF REVERSAL

Our earlier discussion of religion and play included various rites of reversal that are at the same time acts of play. Play may be seen as the reverse of work, but ritual reversals of behavior cover a much broader range than play as a substitution for work. If the customs of all societies of which we have record are considered, almost every imaginable kind of reversal and inversion of ordinary behavior exists as a ritual event. The principle of thought involved is thoroughly familiar in our society in many ideas of binary opposition, that is, in concepts of opposing but complementary elements, such as black and white, good and evil, hot and cold, dark and light, male and female, and positive and negative. The *ying* and *yang* philosophy of China interprets the nature of the entire universe on the basis of such binary opposition.

Ritual behavior of any kind is always somehow extraordinary, and hundreds of societies have hit upon the idea of doing as ritual acts things that reverse or oppose normal procedures and normal values. The customs of reversal are, of course, themselves norms; their special nature is that they oppose the norms applying at other times. Reversals may be only small elements of rites of any class or kind, or they may be the guiding theme of grand festivals. They are included in rites as diverse as funerals, weddings, initiation ceremonies and other rites of passage, cyclic rites, witchcraft, rain ceremonies, and rites propitiating ancestral spirits.

Reversals are also sometimes secular activities, but they are then nevertheless ritualized and extraordinary behavior. The Society of the Contraries, an association of male warriors that existed among a number of Indian societies of the Great Plains of North America, was founded on the theme of reverse behavior. Members of the Society followed highly conventionalized rules of contrary behavior, doing so "ritually" or compulsively in the same sense that we speak of people brushing their teeth "religiously." Some of their acts we may readily see as opposing the norms for the rest of the society. They walked backwards, bathed themselves with dirt or mud instead of water, and said "yes" when they meant "no." Other contrary behavior that less clearly opposes the ordinary was nevertheless contrary. The outstanding trait of members of the Society was an extreme show of fearlessness, to which membership in the society pledged them. Contraries did such things as thrust their hands and arms into containers of boiling water and they were famous, or infamous, for their foolhardy bravery in war. These acts were regarded as extraordinary but not as supernaturalistic behavior.

Most customs of reversal are, however, matters of supernaturalism. They are associated with religious rites in the same way as are singing, dancing, and many other kinds of fundamentally secular behavior, or else they are acts with supernatural significance that are required for certain occasions. No crosscultural compilation of these customs has yet been made, but it is clear that they are abundant in both primitive and civilized societies and were formerly common in Europe. Reversals which are dramatic departures from everyday convention, especially those which have moral significance, have struck the attention of observers most forcibly. Other reversals that are less colorful and lack apparent moral significance have often escaped attention or have not been seen as reversals.

Examples of reversal may be drawn from almost any part of the earth about which detailed, descriptive accounts are available. Information on these rites in societies of sub-Saharan Africa is abundant, and we shall take a representative group of examples from these societies. Prescribed acts that lack apparent or readily apparent moral significance include the wearing of articles of clothing backwards or inside out; prohibitions during ritual periods of scratching, bathing, sitting on mats, touching other people, and sexual intercourse; the requirement that during ritual one must sit with legs straight instead of in the usual folded position; and a custom that the king must wear the humblest clothing instead of his royal garments. At the funeral of a child among the Ashanti (Rattray 1954:60), the parents shaved their heads (a token of joy), dressed in white (an insult at funerals), and ate peanut soup (symbolic of a joyous feast). Other examples among the Ashanti are the playing of discordant music, and the killing and eating of an ox, an act otherwise forbidden and defiling. One of the most common acts of reversal in Africa, which may or may not have moral significance, was ritual transvestism, the wearing of the clothing of the opposite sex.

Elsewhere in the world similar customs are also abundant. Ritual tranvestism and the reversal of ordinary motor habits such as dancing and walking counterclockwise instead of in the normal clockwise direction are common. In Japan, ritual transvestism was once a feature of festival dancing in which entire communities participated and young and old wore the clothing of the opposite sex. Japanese customs at funerals which are observed today require that water be poured with a motion of the hands that is the reverse of the normal, a forward rather than the normal backhand movement, and that the folds of the kimono of the deceased be overlapped in an order that is the reverse of the normal. The modern Ainu of northern Japan follow a custom of placing stockings on a corpse so that the heel is atop the foot. A universal custom of reversal on ritual occasions is the prohibition of work and many other activities of ordinary life.

The most striking ritual reversals have already been briefly discussed in the context of play, customs which seemingly have moral significance. As we shall see, however, judgments of moral significance cannot always be made with certainty. Scatological rites, which center on the use of excrement and urine, are an example.

Rites of this kind were an established feature of the ceremonial calendar of Pueblo Indian societies of the southwestern United States. Male members of certain religious associations gave performances, looked upon by other members of their societies as uproariously funny, in which they consumed the feces of dogs and human beings and drank human urine. Such behavior was ordinarily beyond consideration, needed no prohibitive sanction, and has no apparent moral import. To our eyes, these unspeakable acts may seem immoral because they appear inhuman. To the Pueblo Indians, scatological rites appear not to have been a matter of morality but instead an outrageous example of the amusing theme of antithesis that is richly included in Pueblo rites. Ritual transvestism is also puzzling. When, as in various African societies, women wear the clothing of men or men wear the clothing of women while doing lewd burlesques of the behavior of the opposite sex, it is possible to infer sexual antagonism and thus moral significance. The requirement that young men undergoing rites of coming of age must temporarily wear the clothing of females, a custom also found in African societies, does not easily allow such inferences. This practice may symbolize the entry of the young men into the social world of adult males and the severance of childhood ties with their mothers or the world of women and children.

Many rites of reversal are, however, clearly matters of morality, so regarded by the participatnts. These are the festivals in which all normal conventions are theoretically set aside, when theft, assault, obscenity, and lewdness are encouraged or required, when sexual prohibitions applying at other times are lifted, and when the social hierarchy is turned upside down so that the young berate and insult their elders and commoners insult their rulers. Most anthropological accounts of grand festivals of moral and social inversion come from societies of Africa, but these rites are also well established in European tradition in the Saturnalias of ancient Rome and later practices of Europe which, as we have already noted, linger today in restrained form in the Carnival or Mardi Gras.

In modern Scotland, the New Year's season continues to be a time of festival but secular departure from ordinary behavior. Especially in rural Scotland, the grim Calvinistic dourness of the rest of the year is set aside by drastic reversals. This is a time for drunkenness, bawdiness, flirtations, and sexual freedom, and, as compared with the rest of the year, of unrestrained fun and frolic that strongly opposes the standards of everyday propriety. Institutionalized departures from everyday moral norms that are not in a religious context are also found now and then in primitive society. The holiday known as *pi supuhui*, "a hundred pettings," of the Micronesian island of Ulithi sets aside everyday rules but is not connected with religion (Lessa 1966:84–85). Couples of opposite sex, regardless of age, pair off and go into the woods. Married couples and certain categories of relatives may not go off together. Sexual freedom and merriment follow, and sexual partners are traded. No conflict is reported to result from this institutionalized departure from conventional behavior, which the people describe without apology as "nice play."

The "Feast of Love" or Holī festival of India, a great spring ceremony dedicated to the god Krishna, closely resembles African and old European rites of reversal in which the social and ritual principles of routine life are inverted and each person plays the role of his opposite. Lewdness and sexual license are permitted and expected; some forms of theft are permitted; women beat men with sticks; and members of low castes mix with members of higher castes, sometimes ridiculing and taking other liberties with them. McKim Marriott (1966:200–212), the anthropologist who has given us an eyewitness account of the festivities of Holī, reports many specific inversions. The people who threw mud and dung during the festival were two Brahman priests and a water carrier, experts in daily routines of purification from pollution. The joint singing of three Brahmans, three washermen, and one tailor ignored ideas of inter-caste pollution. Marriott himself, as a man of high social status, was made to dance with a garland of shoes, and a bucket of urine was thrown at him by a woman of low caste. In the eyes of the participants, the festivities of Holī are divine play, "a divine sport of Krishna," and an expression of love for all mankind.

In African rites of reversal, the festival of Holī, and various practices of American Indians, as well as elsewhere in the world, ridicule and questioning of social superiors stands out prominently. In Africa, India, and among the Pueblo Indians, men and women ridicule and sometimes make mock attacks on the opposite sex. Many African societies took their rulers to task during these rites, questioning their competence. American Indian societies of the western United States, and especially the Pueblo Indians, theatrically and hilariously mocked the white man and many other things that were otherwise serious matters. Even religion was mocked. A custom among western Indians was to have a clown parody in burlesque all of the words and acts of a religious specialist performing serious rites. The audience was usually not allowed to laugh. Throughout these rites, an atmosphere of make-believe prevails and this is often expressed by the medium of humor.

Interpreters of this large collection of ritual acts that oppose modes of prevailing behavior see in them many implicit effects or functions. In our earlier discussion of these acts as forms of play, we noted their roles as safety valves and, by dramatizing the everyday norms in reverse and requiring the return to everyday behavior when the festivities end, as reinforcements of the standard rules. We have also noted that all of the reversals may be seen as memorable dramatizations of the events which they celebrate, in this sense having sanctioning force.

Strong social sanction may lie in the many satirical acts of inversion. Reversals in the form of outrageous, satirical burlesques are sometimes consciously aimed at correcting behavior. Marriott reports that among the festivities of Holī were the hanging of festoons of goat bones on the house of a troublesome, litigious widow and the singing of a dirge before the house of an uncharitable moneylender. Among other societies, special rites that depart from normal convention have the specific role of ridiculing and thus seeking to correct undesirable behavior. A ceremony of this kind is followed by the Micronesians of Ulithi in a dance called the *hamath*, which is described as "an outrageously indecorous dance with lewd words" (Lessa 1966:81–82).

This dance is performed on peculiarly disparate occasions, having an inter-connection through their relationship to the great god Iongolap. When used as a corrective it employs songs of criticism by men against women, and vice versa. It is a battle of derogatory taunts which may start against a single individual but ultimately widens its scope so as to become part of the war of the sexes. The words are straight-forward, bitter, and obscene. Thus, if a woman is being attacked, her name is mentioned without evasion, and she may be accused of having an odd-sized sex organ or a large rectum. The dancers may tell how often they have creeped up to her as she lay asleep, and tickled her vagina. She may be accused of masturbating and performing *fellatio*. As the song is being sung, the reason for the attack on the woman is revealed, be it for laziness, shrewishness, adultery, and so on. When women take their turn with the dance they retaliate in kind. Sexual alignments and sexual ridicule play the main part in the performance.

A special interpretation, briefly mentioned in our discussion of play, has been given by Max Gluckman (1954:21) to a part of the rites of reversal, those which, like the *hamath*, express social conflict. Gluckman has given to these ceremonies the name "rituals of rebellion," seeing them as periodic, cathartic expressions of rebellion against authority which, unlike revolt against authority, is only temporary and serves functionally as a social binder. This interpretation stems from theories of the socially supportive functions of conflict, a current of thought with a long history which is wholly in keeping with the prevailing view in social science that any established custom or institution serves functionally to support the social status quo. As we have noted, this interpretation is not well suited for all customs of trans- vestism. It seems peculiarly well suited to the customs of the aboriginal African kingdoms of the Swazi and the Zulu, where, in former times, the rulers were the centers of great annual ceremonies. Among the Zulu, armed warriors dramatically made a mock assault upon the king, leaping from the ranks, denouncing him, blaming his actions, calling them base and cowardly, obliging him to explain, questioning his explanations, and finally threatening and expressing contempt for him. The festival ended with the assemblage of warriors singing a song honoring the country and calling attention to the difficulties the king faces, a song which the ethnologist describing the rite has called a "national anthem" (Samuelson 1929)[2] and which we may see as an affirmation of the normal social order.

The prevalence of ritualized acts that reverse the ordinary is puzzling. Perhaps they represent a universal and innate way of thinking of the human species, a "principle" or "structure" of human thought. In the rites that oppose moral values and the social order, we have no difficulty, however, in seeing the role of religion once again as a channeling device that both permits and controls.

[2] For a similar account of rites of the Swazi, see Kuper (1961) in Recommended Readings.

7

Religious Movements

One of the most remarkable religious phenomena of the past few centuries has been the frequent occurrence throughout most of the world of organized bursts of religious activity. Most of these religious movements have taken place among the culturally simpler societies of the world, after they came into contact with Europeans. As the acts of heathens, the movements were little noted by the Europeans unless they also involved armed resistance to European domination. Scholars of human behavior sometimes described the movements but only tardily recognized them as cultural phenomena of considerable social significance.

As Europeans spread about the globe and militarily, economically, and otherwise dominated the societies with which they came in contact, enormous disorganization of native life occurred. Many societies were wiped out or drastically reduced in size by gunfire, loss of lands or loss of other means of gaining a livelihood, and the spread of diseases brought by the Europeans to which the native people had no immunity. These are all historic events familiar to everyone. Other effects of European contacts with foreign societies are less well known and, for the most part, have been interesting only to scholars. Whether or not the native societies suffered drastic reduction through death, disease, and economic deprivation, they characteristically suffered serious problems of cultural adjustment. Unable to continue the traditional ways of life, they were also unable to make satisfactory transitions to European culture, and often enough were denied the opportunity to do so.

These circumstances are usually described by anthropologists as problems of acculturation, change in culture coming about through the sustained, first-hand contact between societies. Acculturative adjustments of the native societies varied according to differences in their cultures and differences in the strains of European culture to which they were exposed. When European culture was overpowering, a common reaction was demoralization and despair. Another common reaction was a recourse to religion in an attempt at self-help.

The record of acculturative religious movements since the end of the sixteenth century is huge and may readily be correlated with the introduction or imposition of European culture. Early movements are poorly recorded, but many that have developed during the past century are well documented and have been the subjects of anthropological study. Information is most abundant on the reactions of Indian societies of North America, the part of the world which has been the subject of the most intensive anthropological study. As elsewhere, religious movements among the native population of North America followed, after some years, the spread of Europeans. The earliest in the present-day United States occurred among Pueblo Indians of the southwest, who were under Spanish domination. In 1680 the Tewa Indians of present-day New Mexico drove out the Spanish, destroyed all Christian objects, and returned to the native religion. As northern Europeans settled the eastern coast of the United States and moved inland, conquering Indian societies en route, many native religious movements followed in the late seventeenth and early eighteenth centuries. Two of the largest movements, both of which emphasized morality and ritual purification as roads to salvation, arose among the Shawnee and the Iroquois. The Shawnee movement, established on the basis of a prophetic revelation by a former ne'er-do-well who was a brother of the famed Tecumseh, quickly won many converts and was regarded by white colonial administrators as a threat to peace and order. "The Shawnee Prophet," also known by his Indian name of Big Mouth and, later, as Open Door, a name which he adopted after his revelatory experience, had almost instant success as the leader of a feverish movement. A remarkable demonstration by him of his supernatural power quickly won many followers, who spread word of his rare talent. Receiving word of an impending eclipse of the sun, the prophet conducted before an Indian audience a ceremony in which he sternly commanded the sun to darken and to return to brilliance. The sun was seen to follow his bidding.

The early nineteenth century saw movements arise among the small Indian societies of California, who were under Spanish domination. In the late nineteenth century the scene changes to the midwest, the northwest, and the interior of the far west. Outstanding among the developments there were the Shaker Religion of the northwest coast, so called because its ritual activities involved trembling of the limbs; the Ghost Dance Religion, first active in California and later reaching the Great Plains; and the Peyote Religion, which spread widely in the western United States and Canada. Of these movements, the Ghost Dance Religion as such is extinct, although certain of its ritual elements are preserved in other contexts; the Shaker Religion continues to have a small number of adherents, and the Peyote Religion, which we shall later describe in greater detail, is today the largest organized Indian religion of North America.

The religious history of other regions of the world is closely similar. Central and South America saw many native movements, although these are generally only fragmentarily recorded. Native societies of the Pacific Ocean, particularly Melanesia, have also experienced many such episodes. Historic and modern Africa has been the scene of uncounted hundreds of religious movements, many of which have been native versions of Christianity. Of these dozens of movements only two, the Mau Mau Cult of Kenya of the 1950s and the Cargo Cults of Melanesia, have received attention in the international press.

These religious movements all hold much in common although they differ considerably in specific contents and sometimes in specific aims. Anthony Wallace has called them "revitalization movements," a term which seems particularly fitting. All are attempts at self-help at times of crisis. Many have been called "nativistic movements," a term defined as organized movements to revive or perpetuate certain elements of the native culture. But "nativism" seems also to have another definition. For a time, anthropologists tended to call all religious movements of primitive or tribal societies "nativistic", perhaps only because they were something the natives were doing. Many movements did not seek to revive or retain native ways. The nostalgic exaltation of the old, tried, and true is, however, a common theme in these movements and a common theme in any society undergoing socially disruptive cultural change. At least in political matters, this idea is frequently heard in the modern United States.

Many of the movements in primitive societies have been explicitly nativistic. They have tried to regain the old way of life, often attempting to do so by following certain traditional practices of the native religion. The Ghost Dance Religion, as it existed in the Great Plains about 1890, was an attempt to bring back to life the spirits of dead relatives (the ghosts), and to bring back also the vanished buffalo and all of the former Indian way of life. This was to be done wholly by supernaturalism, the performance of a special dance and other prescribed ritual acts.

Religious movements elsewhere among nonliterate societies combine the traditional or native and the new or foreign in both their goals, which are practical secular matters, and their ritual procedures. Some, such as the Cargo Cults, have alternated between the old and the new, changing from native ritual beliefs and procedures to rejection of the native in favor of native versions of Christian procedures, and sometimes later rejecting the Christian in favor of the native.

Religious movements of Africa during the past century have been outstanding in their adaptations of the introduced religions of Islam and Christianity. The twentieth century has seen the fervored conversion of whole communities and large proportions of tribal groups to one or the other of these religions. The rapid conversion to Islam of entire communities, accompanied by the rejection of the traditional faith and the destruction of traditional religious paraphernalia, has been common in Nigeria and other parts of black Africa near the Sahara and northern Africa, where Islam prevails as the religion. During the 1930s, the religion of the Salvation Army took hold rapidly in the Congo—and because of the unrest it appeared to be causing was regarded by colonial administrators as a serious threat to social order. Many features of the Salvation Army were appealing, including its colorful uniforms, stirring music, and, most of all, the native interpretation that membership in the Salvation Army gave absolution from misdeeds and much-needed protection from witches. Following laws laid down by the colonial administrators, the evil actions of witches could no longer be controlled by the traditional practice of subjecting accused witches to the ordeal by poison. Modern Africa is also remarkable in its number of native or separatist Christian churches, in which religious ideology and services are in the hands of native priests. As the years have passed, these nominally Christian religions have taken on the hue of the native religions.

Many religious movements in tribal society have tried to improve the lives of their adherents pacifistically, solely by means of observing traditional or new religious beliefs. But these movements have often involved much more than religious beliefs and acts. Some have physically opposed European domination by warfare. If the entire list of movements is examined, a great mixture in the proportions of secular and supernaturalistic techniques of self-aid are evident. The movements sometimes aim to reject European culture and European people; or, like the Cargo Cults of Melanesia they may try to gain control over European material culture—the goods and products of European societies—rejecting only the European people. Very few of these movements have reached their stated goals, but all may be seen as adaptively useful as courses of action that offer hope when no other recourse seems possible.

Religious movements are, of course, not limited to primitive societies. They are abundant in our own history. Christianity, Judaism, Islam, Buddhism, and all other great religions of the world may be described in various of their phases and sub-phases as religious movements. Religious movements are, in fact, recurrent phenomena in all of the culturally advanced societies of the world which do not prohibit them. Since its founding, the United States has seen dozens of movements, some of which have resulted in established churches. The resident of any sizeable American city is, of course, familiar with small movements that have arisen in recent years. As in tribal society, movements in the United States and other large, industrialized nations are correlated with social disturbances. The United States has seen periods when many religious sects arose and other times when few developed, and these periods of religious activity and quiescence appear clearly to be associated with social unrest in the nation. In nations as large and socially complex as the United States, social unrest has, in fact, become endemic, affecting at any time some part of the population. Religious movements are also endemic, and their teachings and observances reflect the ways of life and the problems of life of their adherents.

In their general nature and goals, the movements of modern literate societies such as the United States do not differ from those of tribal societies. Some may be called nativistic; others are self-consciously "modern." These are intra-societal movements, occurring among segments of a population with many ties to the rest of the people. Perhaps principally for this reason, the movements have seldom involved outright warfare.

A closer look at examples of movements in simple and advanced societies will illustrate their similarities and differences and provide an idea of their range. For this purpose, we have selected three movements that are currently active and one movement of the recent past. The societies these movements represent cover a range extending from a culturally simple tribal group to an advanced urban nation.

THE CARGO CULTS

The Cargo Cults of Melanesia have a history of about one hundred years, during which dozens of movements with diverse ideologies and procedures have risen. All hold in common the goal of attempting to gain control over cargo, the native name, adopted from the English, for ships, airplanes, canned foods, metal tools, automobiles, and all the rest of Western material culture, which first reached the Melanesians as the cargo of ships. The name Cargo Cults was given to these movements in the twentieth century. Many additional names have been given to local developments and to movements of considerable spread that were active for a time and later died out or were replaced by somewhat different ideas and procedures. The movements have been variably nativistic in both contents and aims. In general, they have opposed the foreigners who have had control over them, the British, Dutch, the Japanese during World War II, and the Austrialians who now govern a good part of Melanesia. Although not always militantly antagonistic to their foreign controllers, they have generally included ideas of gaining Melanesian independence. The main outbursts of these movements, which at these times have often risen, spread, changed, and spread again with great speed, occurred during and after World War I and World War II, the times of greatest contact between Melanesians and foreigners.

According to the Melanesian view, the material culture or cargo of the foreigners is provided to the foreigners supernaturally, and Melanesian movements have thus sought to learn and use the supernaturalistic procedures necessary for controlling the cargo. Native interpretations of the nature of the supernatural world are highly personified and concrete, and native interpretation of introduced Christianity follows the indigenous mold. As in aboriginal Melanesian life, much emphasis is placed in the rites of the Cargo Cults upon magical techniques to gain control or to learn the procedures necessary for gaining control, and when these fail to bring results they are quickly replaced by other, essentially identical techniques. Movements are characteristically established by prophets who learn from revelations techniques for gaining control of cargo and ensuring a good life for their followers. Devotional acts to a native supernatural being may be the formula of one revelation. When it seems clear that this formula is unsuccessful, another is tried, which may reject the native gods and appeal to the Christian God. One movement interpreted God as the controller of cargo, stored in great warehouses in the sky above Sydney, Australia, in a supernatural world from which long rope ladders extended to the earth on which spirits of deceased Melanesians climbed as porters, bringing the cargo to earth.

The movements have thus far been unsuccessful in their attempts to gain independence from or equality with the foreigners. Because of the nature of Melanesian societies, prospects for success in the future seem doubtful even if the movements were to include warfare. Melanesia covers a large area of land and ocean, extending from New Caledonia in the south to the Bismarck Archipelago in the north and the Fiji Islands in the east, and including New Guinea. No overall unity exists or has ever existed. (No current information is available on circumstances in West Irian, the large part of New Guinea now controlled by the Republic of Indonesia.) Among the Melanesians in aboriginal times, social unity and amity applied to very small groups. Languages were very diverse and often mutually unintelligible. Especially in New Guinea, neighboring societies only a few miles away often spoke different languages and regarded each other as enemies, suitable targets for practices of headhunting. Regional spreads of prophecies of the Cargo Cults, accomplished through the medium of Pidgin English, have brought together peacefully people that formerly had no amicable contact with each other, but the possibility of a united native Melanesia remains very dim.

THE PEYOTE RELIGION

The Peyote Religion is known more formally by its legal name, the Native American Church, a religious sect that is chartered in many western states of the United States and some of the provinces of Canada. It takes its name from its practices of sacramental use of peyote, *Lophophora williamsii*, a small, spineless species of cactus which grows in Mexico and some parts of the southwestern United States. Supplies of peyote, most commonly "buttons," the dried round tops of the plant, are ordinarily imported from Mexico. Peyote contains the alkaloid substance called mescaline and is customarily called one of the hallucinogenic plants. Peyote alters perception, inducing visions or hallucinations in color, but has no known aftereffects that are harmful.

The beginnings of the Peyote Religion are in ancient Mexico, where peyote was used ritually to induce visions. Its spread to the United States and Canada followed the domination of Indian groups there by white settlers and the disruption of native life. First used by the Apaches of the southwest in the nineteenth century, peyote spread rapidly among Indians of the Great Plains at the end of the century, when native life had ended and the Indians had been placed on reservations. All of the circumstances of suffering and demoralization familiar in the background of these movements elsewhere were present, and the ground was also favorable for the acceptance of the Peyote Religion because of the traditional importance of revelatory visions. With the use of peyote, visionary transcendence was possible for anyone.

Aims of the Peyote Religion are the cultivation of well-being. The religion has always been pacifist. It is nativistic in including native Indian elements in its theology and acts, in being confined almost entirely in its membership to Indians, and in being regarded by its members as an Indian religion. It does not seek to drive out the white man or to bring about any other alteration of society. The dogma and practices of the Peyote Religion are a combination of Christianity and native beliefs. The Christian concepts of God and Jesus Christ are included and the cross is used symbolically. Regularly scheduled rites begin on Saturday night and end Sunday morning. These ceremonies include purification rites, traditionally done by washing oneself with the smoke of burning incense cedar, and, most prominently, the singing of special peyote songs accompanied by drumming. Songs are sung individually and in turn four times—the number four has supernatural significance —by members of the congregation, who are seated in a circle before an altar. Songs are accompanied by drumming, traditionally done on a trade kettle, a cast iron cooking pot, over the mouth of which a drumhead has been stretched. A principal feature of the ceremonies is the consumption of peyote, which, aided by the activities of singing and beating drums and other ritual acts, brings visions. Meetings conclude with a ceremonial breakfast and, later, the informal recounting of visions. Meetings are orderly and include no violent visionary transports.

THE MAU MAU MOVEMENT

The Mau Mau movement of the Kikuyu tribesmen of Kenya in the 1950s was first called a movement of armed revolt and terrorism and only later were its religious elements recognized. The role of religion in the movement was powerful but essentially peripheral. Mau Mau aimed to gain independence from the British and sought to do so principally by armed warfare. All of the familiar conditions for revolt, and for the emergence of a religious movement, existed. The Kikuyu, who gained a livelihood by raising crops and livestock, had lost lands to the British and had suffered a serious drought, invasions of locusts, famines, and epidemics of disease among themselves and their livestock. Native customs clashed in many ways with rules enforced by the British, and much discontent was felt because of British practices of discrimination.

The Mau Mau movement was indeed nativistic, seeking to establish an independent nation with ways of life to be determined by the Kikuyu rather than the British. It is clear, however, from later developments in Kenya that the Kikuyu conception of the good life is not confined to the traditional culture. As one of the newly independent nations of Africa, Kenya combines modernity with tradition.

It is useful to note that the Kikuyu society was relatively sophisticated. Many of its people valued and sought formal education, and its leader, Jomo Kenyatta, had university training in England and long experience with British administrators. Religious aspects of the Mau Mau movement appear to have been deliberately planned. Over the decades many Kikuyu had converted to Christianity and were members of separatist Christian churches. An attempt was made to establish the native faith as the national religion and to incorporate in it the separatist Christian churches. This effort does not seem unrealistic since the dogma of the native religion resembles that of the Old Testament and the separatist churches had taken on features of the native religion.

Most important as a religious element in the Mau Mau movement was the use of traditional oaths that bound members to the movement. These put strong supernatural sanction upon the faithful performance of acts decreed by the leaders as required to reach the goals of the movement. Induction into Mau Mau was an impressive rite of passage, complete with an elaborate ceremony of initiation which included the taking of an oath. Membership in the Mau Mau organization was graded, and so also were oaths, rising in the strength of their sanctions as degree of membership rose. Acts of terrorism included forcing people to take the oaths, and fear of the terrible supernatural punishments incurred by breaking the oaths kept these forced members in the movement. Acts required in the oaths and supernatural sanctions for the oaths increased in horror as the grade of membership rose. For the uppermost of the several grades of membership, oaths were so unspeakably bestial that they are said to have made acts of terrorism and warfare seem mild in comparison.

The Mau Mau movement was forcibly put to an end some years ago, and its leader, Jomo Kenyatta, was imprisoned by the British. If the movement did not by itself reach its goal of gaining independence for the Kikuyu, it seems at least to have made a strong contribution to that end, since Kenya has for some years been an independent nation with Jomo Kenyatta at the head of its government.

THE NEW RELIGIOUS SECTS OF JAPAN

As judged by statistics on the number of people affiliated with organized religious sects, modern Japan is one of the least religious nations of the world. Numerous surveys of the nation inform that only about 30 percent of the people declare themselves as church members. Established religious bodies of the two traditional religions, Shinto and Buddhism, have for many years suffered a growing loss of members and, correspondingly, of financial support. Christianity has a long history in Japan, but if success is measured by the number of adherents, it has been very unsuccessful. Approximately 700,000 people of the nation's population of over one hundred million are members of Christian churches. The general trend in Japan for many years has been a turning away from organized religion. Circumstances behind this trend include the growth and acceptance of scientific views and of scientific procedures, such as in medicine, that have replaced supernaturalism. Perhaps the most important influencing condition has been the rigidity of the old, established sects of Buddhism and Shinto. In theology and practice both religions have been slow to change and they are no longer congruent with conditions of modern life. For example, Japanese Buddhism continues to stress reverence for ancestors, a matter that was formerly very important in Japan and wholly congruent with the social and economic importance of ancestral lines, and much of Shinto ritual revolves about ideas of pollution and practices of agriculture. Under conditions of modern life, ancestral lines and agriculture have lost a great deal of their former importance and supernaturalistic ideas of pollution have become obsolete.

Despite the growing national indifference toward religion, Japan is also the scene today of unusually great religious activity, a development that at first glance seems anomalous. Since the end of World War II, when religious freedom was given to the population, Japan has seen the rapid emergence of hundreds of new religious sects. Of these, about 150 are active today, and, as a group, the adherents of these sects are undoubtedly the most religiously active people of the nation. A handful of the new sects have risen to great size and wealth and have for some years conducted programs of proselytizing outside Japan, in the United States, Brazil, and other countries of South America, and elsewhere in the world, that have had at least token success. Although these sects are identified in Japan as a group as "new sects," very little in their teachings is new. Their dogmas are variously Buddhist, Shinto, and, less often, Christian. Frequently, the sects combine theological elements of these religions together with traces of ancient Taoism and unidentified ideas of supernaturalism that are ancient in Japan. Many sects emphasize faith healing, and reasons for conversion to membership given by the converts themselves include most prominently the attractiveness of promises of cures of illness.

The success of the new sects cannot be explained, however, on the basis of either dogma or faith healing. Like the dogma of the established sects of Buddhism and Shinto, the theology of the new sects is old and, to most of the population of Japan, obsolete. The dogma of Soka Gakkai, the largest of the new sects, a vast organization that claims as many as 20,000,000 adherents and in fact has at least several million members, is a good example. The theology of Soka Gakkai is derived principally from teachings formulated in the thirteenth century that are the official dogma of a Buddhist sect, Nichiren Shoshu, with which Soka Gakkai is loosely associated as a lay body. Nichiren Shoshu was never very successful in attracting adherents. In 1920, the membership of this sect was officially given as 66,000 persons. The Buddhist dogma of Soka Gakkai is, moreover, fundamentally like that of some old Buddhist sects of Japan that have declined in importance. Faith healing is similarly an inadequate explanation of the success of Soka Gakkai or other new sects. Japan is a nation where scientific medicine has long been established and where medicine is socialized and readily available at low cost to most of the population. Faith healing continues to have appeal to those who suffer from scientifically incurable diseases, of course, and some appeal stems from the sect's claim to heal social problems. Relief of distress arising from personal relations with other people and from psychological strain related to excessive drinking, gambling, and other kinds of moral defection are also promised by membership in the sect. But it is impossible to believe that the majority of the several million members of Soka Gakkai, which include a great many healthy young men and women, were attracted to membership by the promise of healing disease or solving social and psychological problems of which the people are consciously aware.

The success of Soka Gakkai and other new sects may be seen to arise from their structure and operation as social units which are peculiarly well suited to the conditions of modern life as these conditions apply among their adherents. Adherents are drawn from the lower social and economic strata of the nation. As a group, they may be described as the urban proletariat of Japan, people employed in industry or following other occupations associated with industry who have adequate incomes for a moderately comfortable life but who are seldom well-to-do or rich and who, characteristically, have had little or no advanced formal education and little or no exposure to scientific philosophy. The dogma of the new sects is then acceptable to them and, what is most important to them, membership in the sects offer psychological and social rewards that are difficult for these people to gain otherwise under conditions of modern Japanese life.

During the past century, economic and associated social changes in Japan have been drastic. One of the most striking social changes has been a decline in the size and importance of kin groups, through membership in which all of the important activities of life were formerly conducted. The modern Japanese family is characteristically the nuclear family of parents and children, and ties with relatives outside this group have weakened as industrialization has allowed individuals to be economically independent. A traditional feature of Japanese personality and society which continues to have great strength today is a strong social and emotional dependence upon others. Much more than citizens of the United States, the Japanese are joiners, who seek social identification and affectively important relationships with others through membership in groups. For the economically and educationally favored classes, such social identification is provided through the normal activities of life. Japanese industrial firms typically cultivate the ingroup sentiment among their salaried employees, providing satisfying identification as members of the group. For the rank and file of industrial employees, social identification through their employment is weak, and opportunities to gain such identity outside their places of employment are few. Membership in the new religious sects provides the desired social identification, and the modes of organization and activities of the sects are extraordinarily effective in simultaneously meeting the needs of individual members and reaching organizational goals.

In the range of their activities, the large new sects of Japan must surely be the most remarkable religious organizations of industrialized society. The convert is firmly embedded in the organization by a complex of activities that enters into almost every aspect of human life. Hierarchy exists in the organization for reaching organizational goals, but, at the same time, hierarchy is balanced by strong egalitarianism. Soka Gakkai and all other large new sects have what may be called vertical and horizontal lines of organization, skillfully balanced. Horizontal, egalitarian organization is through an elaborate network of subassociations concerned with sports, all branches of art and esthetics, education, and politics, and also by a small-group organization that, in a warm atmosphere of sympathy and solidarity, encourages members to discuss personal problems and seek their solution with the aid of counsellors who guide the sessions. The activities of the sects are placed principally in the hands of members, and only a proportionately tiny number of administrators draw their livelihood from sect finances. Both the religious and the secular activities of the sects embed and reward members, and the secular subgroups connected with sports, esthetic pursuits, and the like offer the richest opportunities for pleasurable and socially satisfying activities. Sporting meets of the youth organizations of Soka Gakkai are grand affairs, so heavily attended that they must be conducted in the largest stadiums in the nation. Identification with one's sect is also strongly fostered by lavish use of visible and audible symbols of membership and unity, which include badges, special songs, drum and fife bands, and extremely elaborate religious edifices that are heavily used for meetings.

Most of the population of Japan looks upon the new religious sects with suspicion and with at least mild contempt. The sects unquestionably provide important psychological and social regards for their members—and one may ponder their social value to the entire society. Some fear exists in the nation over the possibility of Soka Gakkai's gaining totalitarian control over the nation, especially because of its political success in putting sect members into many elective offices in the national Diet and in local governing bodies. At least in the past, alarm was also felt over the sect's practices or alleged practices of forced conversion. As safety valves alleviating the distresses of their members which might otherwise be disruptive to the nation, the new sects may be seen as contributing to national social harmony. From a scholarly viewpoint, these sects seem in one respect to be unique. No other industrial, scientifically advanced nation of the world provides a comparable example of the penetration of religion deeply into the lives of a substantial part of the population.

8

The Past and the Future

In the preceding chapters, two themes or principles of organization have been followed, sometimes separately and sometimes jointly. We have discussed the anthropological study of religion, how anthropologists have gone about studying this subject, and the assumptions upon which their interpretations have been based. We have also discussed the ideas and acts of religion in many societies of the world, calling attention to similarities and differences. Both the study of religion and religion itself continue, and our concluding remarks will concern the past and the future of both.

Reviewing the foregoing pages, we may see certain trends and assumptions of the anthropological study of religion that merit special note. Perhaps the most outstanding trait is the implicit anthropological assumption that, although social malfunctioning may occur at times of great cultural change, the positive or supportive effects of religious beliefs and acts outweigh their negative or disruptive effects. Using other terminology, we may say that anthropological interpretations have given great emphasis to the positive, implicit functions of religion. This tendency, we may also note, follows or accords with the anthropological assumption that culture is composed of a system of congruent, mutually supportive elements. No quantitative procedures have been devised for objectively weighing positive against negative, and it seems probable that few persons have thought such an undertaking either feasible or desirable.

A related anthropological assumption evident in our discussions of many topics of religion is that the place of religion in the system of culture is essentially derivative, that is, that religion takes its specific form and content from nonreligious sectors of human experience and serves principally in a supportive role. This statement does not, however, deny that religious beliefs and acts once instituted may have profound effects upon the rest of culture or that religion often appears to be the effective source of human motivation.

We may note also that the great majority of interpretative anthropological studies of religion of the past few decades have concerned the relationship between religion and the social order, and have much less frequently or directly concerned other parts of culture such as technology, economics, or structured modes of thinking that pervade all cultural activities of a society. In keeping with the anthropological emphasis upon groups and modes, relatively little attention has been given to the individual and to the subject of psychological functions of religion. Every category of the anthropological study of religion that we have discussed does indeed include implicit or explicit ideas of psychological tensions to which the religious beliefs and acts relate, but the focus of study has been the cultural—primarily the social—circumstances producing inferred stresses rather than the psychological processes or dynamisms involved. The prevailing functionalist view of religion as a dynamic system of social action and the methodologically congruent emphasis upon observation of social matters may be said to have had another largely unintended effect, the relative neglect of dogma, mythology, and various other aspects of symbolism.

A recent trend of interpretation, which resembles and is perhaps historically related to modern interests in perception and cognition, returns to the study of symbolism, seeking to understand the underlying principles or structure of religion as expressed in the symbols of dogma, mythology, and ritual. These studies have often found in the symbols coherent schemes of binary opposition. We have earlier noted that this relationship seems evident in rituals of reversal.

Other trends and horizons of the anthropological study of religion are worthy of mention. Increasing attention is being given to culturally elaborate civilizations of the world. A concomitant interest is evident in questions of current interest in international relations, such as the role of religion in human motivation toward achievement, a subject previously left principally to psychology and sociology. The study of rituals of reversal remains a frontier, and the future will doubtless see additional investigation of this subject. A related subject which we have discussed remains on the scholarly horizon. This is the anthropological study of human play, a topic which has obvious bearings on much religious activity, perhaps particularly rites of reversal and the factors involved in motivation toward economic and general cultural development. Related to play is humor, an important aspect of the ceremonies of many primitive societies but a subject of which social science has yet gained little knowledge and which, in its relationship to religion, appears hardly to have reached the horizons of anthropology. It is evident, however, that humor is an important feature of many religious rites.

These remarks about trends for the future contain a note of hope for the future anthropological study of religion. Research of the past and the influence of research in other fields have stimulated the formulation of new questions and new approaches to gaining answers. If, as is often maintained, heuristic value is a measure of scientific worth, the future seems hopeful. It is evident that old research and old conclusions have not been abandoned, and that the frontiers of study make use of them in seeking added understanding of the nature of religion.

If we now consider the roles of religion in human life, as illustrated or interpreted in the foregoing accounts, we must conclude that religion has played a vital part. Our examination of religious circumstances in culturally simple societies brings out clearly its pervasive influence in these societies. In such activities of life as economic work, play, and the handling of illness, in which it scarcely plays vital roles in our own society today, religion has in the past served man when no other interpretations and courses of action were available. In much of man's history, religion has entered into every aspect of life. The past few centuries have seen a progressive shrinking of its sphere of activities, accompanied by a reinterpretation of religion that alters or eliminates anthropocentric conceptions of supernatural beings and, in our society, gives greatest stress to the moral value of religion. The transition has not been entirely smooth. We have now and then called attention to some of the problems that the relinquishing of old religious customs has brought. In matters of social and moral deviance from approved standards, for example, explanations of deviation tend increasingly to represent the viewpoints of the social sciences. In our own society, no wholly satisfactory secular substitutes for the sanctioning force of religion in moral matters have yet developed. The culturological or sociological explanations current today of the conditions that foster crime, violence, juvenile delinquency, and other socially disruptive behavior have presented us with serious problems of judging culpability for such disruptive acts which the traditional and, in the opinion of many, outmoded moral-religious attitudes toward social deviance did not present. This is to say, once again, that the transition from primitive to modern conditions has brought problems as well as benefits for mankind. As for the future of religion, the conclusion also seems clear. Religious ideology and ritual have undergone much change in the past few centuries and evidence of continuing change is abundant. There seems little doubt that religion, much altered in various of its aspects in keeping with other trends of change, will long endure.

Recommended Readings

Banton, Michael, ed., 1966, *Anthropological Approaches to the Study of Religion.* London: Tavistock Publications.

Berkowitz, M. I., and J. E. Johnson, eds., 1900, *Social Scientific Studies of Religion: A Bibliography.* Pittsburgh: University of Pittsburgh Press.

Durkheim, Émile, 1954, *The Elementary Forms of the Religious Life.* New York: The Free Press. (Translation from the French, originally published in 1912.)

Evans-Pritchard, E. E., 1965, *Theories of Primitive Religion.* Oxford: Clarendon Press.

Frazer, J. G., 1928, *The Golden Bough*, one vol., abridged. New York: The Macmillan Company.

Geertz, Clifford, 1960, *The Religion of Java.* New York: The Free Press.

Gluckman, Max, 1954, *Rituals of Rebellion in South-East Africa.* Manchester: University of Manchester Press.

Goode, William J., 1951, *Religion among the Primitives.* New York: The Free Press.

Kluckhohn, Clyde, 1944, *Navaho Witchcraft.* Papers of the Peabody Museum of American Archaeology and Ethnology, Vol. 22, No. 2.

Kuper, Hilda, 1961, *An African Aristocracy.* London: Oxford University Press.

Leach, Edmund, ed., 1967, *The Structural Study of Myth and Totemism.* London: Tavistock Publications.

Malefijt, Annemarie de Waal, 1968, *Religion and Culture, An Introduction to the Anthropology of Religion.* New York: The Macmillan Company.

Malinowski, Bronislaw, 1948, *Magic, Science and Religion and Other Essays.* New York: The Free Press. (Republication of earlier writings.)

Marriott, McKim, 1966, "The Feast of Love," *in* Milton Singer, ed., *Krishna: Myths, Rites and Attitudes.* Honolulu: East-West Center Press.

Middleton, John, ed., 1967, *Gods and Rituals, Readings in Religious Beliefs and Practices.* Garden City, N.Y.: The Natural History Press.

Norbeck, Edward, 1961, *Religion in Primitive Society.* New York: Harper & Row.

Norbeck, Edward, 1970, *Religion and Society in Modern Japan: Continuity and Change.* Rice University Studies, Vol. 56, No. 1 (whole number); hardcover edition, Houston: Tourmaline Press.

Radcliff-Brown, A. R., 1952, *Structure and Function in Primitive Society.* New York: The Free Press. (Republication of earlier writings.)

Rattray, R. S., 1954, *Religion and Art in Ashanti.* London: Oxford University Press.

Samuelson, R. C. A., 1929, *Long, Long Ago.* Durban, Knox Printing and Publishing Co. (Translated from Delegorgue, M. A., *Voyage dans l'Afrique Australe*, 2 vols. Paris: Au Dépôt de Librairie, 1847.)

Tyler, Stephen A., 1973 (reissued 1986), *India: An Anthropological Perspective.* Prospect Heights, IL: Waveland Press, Inc.

Tylor, E. B., 1889, *Primitive Cultures*, 2 vols., 3d American ed. New York: Henry Holt and Co. (First published 1871).

van Gennep, Arnold, 1960, *The Rites of Passage.* Chicago: The University of Chicago Press. (Translation from the French, originally published in 1909.)

Wallace, Anthony F. C., 1966, *Religion: An Anthropological View.* New York: Random House.

White, Leslie A., 1959, *The Evolution of Culture.* New York: McGraw-Hill Book Co.

Whiting, J. M., R. Kluckhohn, and A. Anthony, 1958, "The Functions of Male Initiation Ceremonies at Puberty," *in* Maccoby, E. E., T. M. and E. L. Hartley, eds., *Readings in Social Psychology*, 3d ed. New York: Holt, Rinehart and Winston, Inc.

Young, Frank W., 1965, *Initiation Ceremonies, A Cross-Cultural Study of Status Dramatization.* New York: The Bobbs-Merrill Co.

Religion in Specific Societies

Each of the works listed and annotated below are available in paperback from Waveland Press. They provide specific information on features of religion and offer anthropological interpretations of the functional significance of these elements. As examples of religious customs of individual societies, they serve both to illustrate and to provide additional information on the subject of religion. Priced reasonably, these titles are excellent for supplementary reading in a variety of courses.

Africa
- [ ] Bascom, **The Yoruba of Southwestern Nigeria**
- [ ] Gamst, **The Qemant: A Pagan-Hebraic Peasantry of Ethiopia**
- [ ] Harris, **Casting Out Anger: Religion among the Taita of Kenya**
- [ ] Schaffer-Cooper, **Mandinko: The Ethnography of a West African Holy Land**

Asia
- [ ] Fraser, **Fishermen of South Thailand**
- [ ] Preston, **Cult of the Goddess: Social and Religious Change in a Hindu Temple**

Europe
- [ ] Messenger, **Inis Beag: Isle of Ireland**

Latin America
- [ ] Bastien, **Mountain of the Condor: Metaphor and Ritual in an Andean Ayllu**
- [ ] Nash, **In the Eyes of the Ancestors: Belief and Behavior in a Mayan Community**

North America
- [ ] Basso, **The Cibecue Apache**
- [ ] Jones, **Sanapia: Comanche Medicine Woman**
- [ ] Williams, **Community in a Black Pentecostal Church: An Anthropological Study**

Pacific
- [ ] Hicks, **Tetum Ghosts and Kin**
- [ ] Lessa, **Ulithi: A Micronesian Design for Living**

Questions and Topics for Discussion

PART I INTRODUCTION: THE ANTHROPOLOGICAL
STUDY OF RELIGION

Chap. 1 *The Nature of Religion: Anthropological Views*

1. How can the universality of religion be explained? Is the explanation biological or cultural? If biological, how can the existence of nonreligious people in our society be explained?
2. Without reading beyond this chapter, what explanations can you offer of the significance of the several strange customs described in the opening pages?
3. As compared with other scholarly fields, what is distinctive about anthropology in its studies of religion?
4. State your own definition of religion, or ask a friend to do so. Ask yourself whether or not this definition is suitable for all other societies. If not, why is it unsuitable?
5. Do you regard the supernaturalistic concepts of Christianity or Judaism as predominantly personified or as impersonal? Explain.
6. How may magic be distinguished from religion?
7. Explain the following: Religion is an element of the system called culture.
8. Give an example of a positive, implicit function of a religious event, such as ceremonies of inauguration, thanksgiving, and funerals.

Chap. 2 *Religious Beginnings*

1. How may Sigmund Freud's ideas of the genesis of religion and E. B. Tylor's views of the evolution of religion be seen as ethnocentric conceptions?
2. What characteristics do magic and science hold in common and how do they differ?
3. Examine the characteristics of the supernatural beings of ancient Greece, Rome, or Egypt, or any other society of the distant past in the Western world. How may the supernatural beings be seen as congruent with the cultures of their times and incongruent with modern ways of life?
4. Give one example of each of the types of magic. Among these types, which is the most common in our society today? What reasons can be given for its popularity?
5. In man's ordinary experiences in life, what things and events may be seen as secular analogies of ideas of impersonal supernatural power and associated acts of magic?
6. How may the ideas of impersonal power of India and of aboriginal Polynesia be seen to provide support for the social hierarchies of these societies?
7. Explain the following: According to Émile Durkheim, the practices of totemism symbolically represent society worshipping itself.
8. What evidence has led archeologists to conclude that the forms of art of prehistoric man of late Paleolithic times in Europe often had supernatural significance?

PART II THE ROLES OF RELIGION IN HUMAN LIFE

Chap. 3 *Introduction*

1. From the viewpoint of planning remedial action, how do educated citizens of our nation today view social problems such as alcoholism and crime? Are these primarily moral problems, related or unrelated to religion, or are they regarded as the expectable results of sociocultural circumstances? What trends of change in interpretation seem evident?

2. How may the assumptions and procedures of the anthropological study of religion be seen as a part of a general trend of change in the interpretation of human behavior that is in keeping with the circumstances relating to Question 1? What role does culture have in these various interpretations?

Chap. 4. *Manners, Morals, and Supernatural Sanctions*

1. Do the illegality, immorality, and sinfulness of polygamy spring entirely from religion? If so, or if not so, how could the proscription of plural marriages have become a religious tenet?
2. In our society, what sanctions apply when an extremely serious crime or sin, such as murder, is committed? Among the population as a whole, what appears to be the relative strength of religious versus secular sanctions for this offense?
3. Do the moral standards of religious and nonreligious people in our society differ? If so, how?
4. Discuss the problem of weighing the positive or socially supportive effects of beliefs and practices of witchcraft against its negative or socially disruptive effects.
5. Witches may be seen as projections on a supernatural plane of what human emotions?
6. What concept of supernatural power is involved in the examples provided in this chapter of supernatural sanctions for breaches of etiquette?
7. What are sumptuary laws? Do any such laws, *de facto* or *de jure*, exist in our society? Are such laws congruous or incongruous with our social organization and political ideals?
8. Why does adherence to rules of etiquette relating to one's kinsmen have such great social importance in primitive societies?

Chap. 5 *Transcendence*

1. In our own society, which are acceptable and which are unacceptable ways of seeking transcendence? What variations exist according to social class, age, and sex?
2. Explain the following statement: In man's history, much human behavior that we today commonly regard as indicating psychological instability has been religiously valued and put to religious and social use.
3. Give examples of "the cultural conditioning of ecstatic states."
4. Describe the procedures and the goals of the vision quest of American Indians of the Great Plains in aboriginal times.
5. Explain the statement that religion has often served as both a channel for and a means of control of transcendental states.
6. What forms of play are generally approved and disapproved in our society? How do these attitudes relate to Protestant views of morality?
7. Using historical information on former circumstances in Western societies and information on primitive societies (as representing the ancient past), contrast the roles of religion as a vehicle for human entertainment in A) the ancient past, B) the historic past of the Western world, and C) modern times in our society.
8. What are rites of reversal and how may they be seen as examples of binary opposition?

Chap. 6 *Group Rites*

1. How do rites of passage and cyclic rites differ and how are they similar?
2. What kinds of rites of passage are commonly observed in the modern United States as religious observances, as secular observances, and as either secular and religious observances or perhaps both?
3. Discuss the types and the significance of the symbols commonly associated with rites of passage.
4. What interpretation may be offered of the functional significance of ordeals at coming of age, such as the example of a requirement that girls catch water bugs in their mouths?

5. What interpretation does anthropology offer of the functional significance of the "classic couvade"?
6. How may simple rites of marriage and divorce be seen as congruous with conditions of life in matrilineal societies and incongruous with circumstances in patrilineal societies?
7. How may the medical practices of primitive societies be seen as linked with ideas of pathogenesis?
8. Which of the medical practices of primitive societies survive today in modern garb?
9. Give examples of rites of reversal with and without apparent moral significance.
10. Explain the following statement: Institutionalized expressions of conflict, such as exist in certain rites of reversal, may be seen to have positive functional value with reference to society.

Chap. 7   *Religious Movements*

1. Discuss the relationship between acculturative stress and religious movements among tribal societies during the past two centuries.
2. Give examples of religious movements among Indian societies of the present-day United States, linking these with problems of acculturation during the past two centuries.
3. How do nativistic movements differ from other religious movements?
4. Give examples from your own knowledge of modern religious movements among the dominant population of the United States and discuss circumstances that appear to have fostered their emergence.
5. Describe the Cargo Cults, including in your description a statement of the manner in which they reflect native views of the world and native supernaturalism.
6. Discuss the moral and legal issues involved in the ritual procedures of the Native American Church.
7. Why do the new religious sects of Japan seem anomalous and what circumstances appear to have fostered their development?
8. Using the principal examples provided in your reading, describe the range of activities, religious and nonreligious, that have been included under the name of religious movements.

Chap. 8   *The Past and the Future*

1. In the anthropological study of religion, what circumstances might account for the emphasis upon the positive, implicit functional aspects of religion?
2. In addition to an emphasis upon positive, implicit functions, what other trends or emphases have characterized the anthropological study of religion?
3. Use the set of values called the Protestant ethic to support the idea that, once instituted, religious beliefs and values may have profound effects upon the rest of culture.
4. What aspects of religion have anthropological studies of religion tended to slight?
5. What are the new trends in the anthropological study of religion?
6. Summarize the anthropological view of the principal roles of religion in human life.